Eduard C. Lindeman

AND SOCIAL WORK PHILOSOPHY

Eduard C. Lindeman

AND SOCIAL WORK PHILOSOPHY

by Gisela Konopka

THE UNIVERSITY OF MINNESOTA PRESS
Minneapolis

Printed in the United States of America at
North Central Publishing Company, St. Paul

Library of Congress Catalog Card Number: 58-9162

PUBLISHED IN GREAT BRITAIN, INDIA, AND PAKISTAN BY THE OXFORD UNIVERSITY PRESS,
LONDON, BOMBAY, AND KARACHI AND IN CANADA BY THOMAS ALLEN, LTD., TORONTO

TO MY PARENTS

who many years ago made great personal and financial sacrifices in order to give their children an education, and who, beyond this, made them feel the beauty of books, learning, and thinking.

ACKNOWLEDGMENTS

T HE acknowledgments for such a book as this should include all the significant people in my life — and there are many. I can name here only those who directly helped to make this inquiry possible.

My first thanks go to Drs. Nathan Cohen, Gordon Hamilton, and Henry Steele Commager who gave generously of their time for reading and discussing the manuscript and who made helpful suggestions for changes.

My thanks also go to all those friends, relatives, and colleagues of Eduard C. Lindeman who allowed me to interview them and who shared written material about him — especially to Mrs. Eduard C. Lindeman who patiently answered many personal questions; to Dr. Robert Gessner and Mrs. Doris Lindeman Gessner who let me spend untold hours in their apartment reading unpublished material by Lindeman; to Mrs. Betty Lindeman Leonard whose enthusiastic response to my intention of writing about her father encouraged me greatly, and who kindly permitted me to quote from letters and other unpublished materials in her possession; to Mrs. Laura Richardson Pratt for the same encouraging response and for financial help; and to Miss Henrietta Dekan who, in her capacity as former secretary to Lindeman, gave me quiet and warm support.

Thanks are due also to the Columbia University Press, publishers of Reinhold Niebuhr's *Contribution of Religion to Social Work*; to Longmans, Green & Co., Inc., publishers of Mary Parker Follett's *The New State*; and to the Association Press, Inc., publishers of Lindeman's *The Community* for permission to quote from their publications.

This undertaking as part of my doctoral work was made possible only through the generous financial help of the Florina Lasker Fellowship and the grant of a Sabbatical Leave by the University of Minnesota. My research could not have been done without the constant and efficient help of the librarians of the New York School of Social Work.

My warmest thanks go to my husband, Erhardt Paul Konopka, whose patient acceptance of long working hours and unshaken faith in my capacity in spite of my own doubts have always helped me to continue and finish a given task.

G.K.

January 1958

CONTENTS

CONTENTS

Eduard C. Lindeman
AND SOCIAL WORK PHILOSOPHY

"THE philosophical basis of social work, with its emphasis upon the value of the individual, still lacks rigorous analysis at the hands of the profession before it can serve as a useful criterion for social evaluation in a democratic society where a fine balance has continually to be struck between the rights of individuals and the interests of the larger group." Ernest V. Hollis and Alice Taylor, *Social Work Education in the United States*, p. 114.

INTRODUCTION: THE IMPORTANCE OF A
PHILOSOPHY FOR SOCIAL WORK

THE nations of the world are engaged in a race for technical supremacy. What is the principal purpose of the race? To prevent one nation — one part of humanity — from dominating or destroying another.

Much intelligence and much energy are going into this effort. Yet it seems more important than ever that an even greater effort be made to achieve positive and mutually helpful human relations. This cannot be accomplished by harnessing technical forces, but only through man himself, working with other men.

Among several others, the profession of social work makes an effort to improve human relations. And today its goals and value system need greater clarification and thinking through by members of the profession.

Certain basic questions constantly recur. What are our explicit goals? How do we relate to present-day society, its problems, and its future development? How do we get away from the mechanical teaching of methods and skills? Do we teach a value system? Which? Why? What are the consequences if we do not do it?

As Nathan Cohen pointed out, we should

ask the question of whether we in our attempt to develop a more scientific professional practice are running the danger of moving toward a "conscienceless scientism." As we have become more and more immersed in developing professional practice, have we kept pace with training for professional responsibilities as well, and for furthering and developing social work goals and objectives and not just the social worker? Is it enough for social workers to be only

3

skillful in the diagnosis and treatment of the individual and group problems which he meets in day to day practice? Doesn't the accomplishment of social work goals and objectives call for a social worker who can also speak with knowledge and understanding of the wider issues involved and the value principles underlying them, and with authority in possible courses of action and development for society as a whole, that is, on social policies?

He put these questions into terms relating to practice:

How can the idealistic values of liberty, fraternity, dignity and equality be given an increasing empirical meaning and content? How can we make moral values more than the outside slices of a sandwich which has as its main ingredients technical skills? And how can we make these values part of the social worker's muscles?

and relating to the teaching of social work:

1. Is the subject matter of social philosophy dealt with as required material or merely as occasional and unplanned content in non-required courses?

2. Are the teachers of technical courses encouraged to emphasize value principles underlying the social work approach?

3. Is reference made to the impossibility of achieving sound social work practice in settings which violate major value principles?

4. Are the practices pertaining to admission, faculty employment and field work placements such that we are providing a proper climate for learning democratic values?

5. If there are gaps between our objectives and social values, and practice, are we focusing on methods and techniques for closing the gap? [1]

How basic those questions were was brought home in 1955 at a meeting of the Council of Social Work Education in the workshop on research. Here were brought together people of the profession selected for their great knowledge of practice, teaching, and research. When they were asked to point out what they considered the burning question in research, their responses covered a wide range; but discussion centered on the *core content* of knowledge for social workers — which automatically brings up the question of *goals* and *values.*

[1] Nathan E. Cohen, "Desegregation — A Challenge to the Place of Moral Values in Social Work Education," *Education for Social Work*, Council on Social Work Education (New York, 1955), pp. 17, 23.

And this concern with goals and values was not new. In studying the history of social work we find repeated over and over again, yet answered differently in different periods of its development, such basic questions as

1. Is social work palliative only or is it responsible also for changing social institutions?

2. What is the definition of the needs and rights of human beings?

3. What is the theory of "adjustment" in relation to social work philosophy?

4. What are social work's specific methods in relation to its value system?

5. How do we combine the concepts of self-determination and planning?

6. What is social work's relation to other professions?

7. What is the relation of the professional to the volunteer?

As early as 1923, in his report on social work education, James H. Tufts posed these questions.

Accepting as fairly well defined a considerable central group of activities, how far may social work wisely extend to various specified border fields . . . how deep shall it go in its exploration and its methods of treatment or prevention? . . . Accepting as undoubtedly necessary a certain type of training for the fairly well-defined agencies of relief, aid and administration or oversight, shall the institutions engaged in giving preparation stop with this conception of their task or shall they aim at so broad and thorough an education and training for at least a minority of their pupils as shall fit them for the larger and profounder tasks which may be conceived under the analogy of social engineering or social statesmanship? Shall they undertake study of the fundamental forces of human life, of the ultimate values of human welfare, and of the great institutions of human society in order to meet that larger responsibility which no other profession than social work at present seems to accept? [2]

We know that these questions are still unanswered, and this calls for at least an attempt to clarify the philosophical system of social work — an attempt which includes its values and goals (including

[2] James H. Tufts, *Education and Training for Social Work* (New York: Russell Sage Foundation, 1923), pp. xi–xii.

responsibilities), its concept of society, its picture of the individual man, and its means and methods.

Why is this necessary? Why can't this profession rely on the influence of cultural pressures and the general thinking of the times? Why must a specific effort be made in the case of social work?

Under the influence of the scientific orientation of the twentieth century, social workers thought they could separate value judgments from the problems presented to them. They thought it sufficient to have an ethical code themselves, while they tried to regard the client and his problem in a dispassionate, scientific way that would not involve a decision about values. This did not work and it cannot work. I will give some practical examples.

1. A social worker is working in a child guidance clinic with a small group of emotionally disturbed pre-school children. Doesn't this look like the simple problem of helping to remove emotional blocks, of working toward health which is in general an uncontested value? Yet — in the course of the group play the social worker is confronted with one child's deep resentment of his parents because they segregate him from other children for religious reasons, and with another child who has early in life been hurt because he is a member of a minority group. In what direction must treatment go? Should it work toward "adjusting" the child to his given status or should it help him to be able some day to fight this status? Even in this small group the question arises: On what value principles should a social worker act?

2. A migrant family comes to the office of the social worker in a border town in one of our states. Since they have no legal residence in any of the forty-eight states, the social worker can provide them with quarters for a few days and can listen to their problems; but at the end of the few days, she has to urge them to move on. Yet — the social worker sees that these are children who do not get schooling, who feel inferior, and whose resentment is beginning to show in small delinquent acts. Is this only a question of juvenile delinquency? Or is the social worker faced with the whole question of federal-state relationships and of planning for welfare? Again there is no escape from acting on the basis of a value system.

3. The social worker in Egypt is confronted with the problem of helping the Arab fellaheen with health problems and child rearing. He has understood one of social work's principles: "to start where the people are"; he knows the situation among the fellaheen and can feel their problems himself. Yet — they actually do not care about modern health practices. Methods based on superstitions are satisfactory to them. What right has the social worker to introduce his value system? What are his goals for such a community and is he allowed to have goals *for* people if he at the same time adheres to the idea of self-determination? Even the community organizer cannot avoid clarifying such conflicts in his value system.

4. The Jewish population of a middle-sized American city has lived in one part of the city for a generation or so and has established there the traditional services, among them a Jewish Center. The younger families begin to move out of this area into a more modern and religiously mixed suburb of the city. Recreational facilities and helpful social activities are inadequate for all the children of this suburb. Some members of the Jewish community strongly feel the need for such service to their children and want to combine it with emphasis on their Jewish heritage. They call on the social worker– community planner to help them with solution of a dilemma: They are not sure whether it is right to establish a separate Jewish center because of the objections of two groups which present two very different points of view. One of the groups represents an orthodox Jewish religious view and thinks it more important that the children keep close contact with the synagogues in the old neighborhood. The other group, a very liberal religious group, thinks it wrong to establish a separate Jewish center because this may perpetuate segregation. They think it more important to help the rest of the community to understand the values of group work and recreational experiences. Obviously the social worker cannot help solve these problems without serious inquiry into different value systems.

5. A young social worker had worked with an aged client and had helped her greatly. When the older woman brought to an interview a scarf she had knitted and offered it to the young worker as a token of her appreciation, the worker accepted, feeling that the

client gained much self-esteem by being able to give something to the worker who had given her so much. She was severely reprimanded by her supervisor who insisted that no gifts should be accepted. Had the supervisor examined her value system to see whether it was consistent with the principle of the dignity of men, expressed in a human wish for mutual giving and accepting?

6. A young widow with a school-age child came to the agency asking for day care for her son so that she could go to the university and prepare for a profession she felt especially qualified for. The agency refused help with placement because it put more importance on a mother's staying home with her child than on her fulfilling her need for professional education. Which value system had been used to make this decision?

The importance of this struggle with values in a profession confronted daily with the practical application of a general philosophy was well expressed in a letter from a young Japanese social worker to her social work teacher in the United States.

There is something going wrong in Japanese society today. I do not know exactly what and how it happened. Many students with whom I am working blindly believe that they can change the whole society within a short time. They think they are completely different from the older generation which can be of no help to them to bring about the "new society." Within the last few weeks more than seven cases of commitment of suicide by young children (ages 7 to 15) are reported . . . Some people think that the YWCA is "radical" because we send out open letters to the world about the atomic and hydrogen bomb. . . . Some think it is too conservative because we did not cooperate with the movement to sign the Vienna Appeal.

"To be non-judgmental" and at the same time, to keep one's own value system clearly with integrity is very difficult when I myself do not know exactly which way to go. It is hard to be the representative of the agency when members have so much difference in opinion as what we as the organization should do. And it is next to impossible to "make a realistic decision" when nobody is sure about what the real situation is today. Here in Japan people with different ideologies give out so different descriptions of what the "real" situation is. In the meantime I made up my mind to work hard to bring about an atmosphere in which people are treated as people — with love and real thoughtful concern. . . . As long as there are people who live together with so many hopes, joy, dreams, disappointment, fear, courage, love, there must be a job for social workers to be called upon.[3]

Because of the difficulty of applying ethical demands to actual situations and the difficulty of evaluating real situations, the questions raised by this letter can never be altogether satisfactorily answered. Neither social work nor philosophy will ever be able to establish rules of conduct applicable to every case. What must be done is to clarify general philosophy and make a constant awareness of his value system a habit of mind for every social worker.

Social work's need to clarify values is so great because its core is *relationships* between human beings; social workers cannot be only scientific observers but must be active conditioners and helpers.

Like all professions, social work grew out of certain needs in society, the needs of the "disadvantaged," those who, for various reasons, could not provide for themselves. In the beginning it served mainly the poor, but with changing social organization, standards changed and different services became necessary. As Eduard Lindeman said, "It is no more the question of raising the standard of living but life itself must be elevated." The problems that present-day social workers deal with, therefore, range from provision of basic necessities such as housing or clothing, on to the problems of bewildered parents and children, old people who feel left out, those forgotten in mental hospitals and prisons, handicapped children and adults, those discriminated against because of race or creed or nationality, and finally to problems related to the free interaction of people for democratic goals. Wherever human institutions or human relations either break down or threaten to break down or are not at the stage of maximum potential, social work has a function to fulfill. There are other professions which are also guided by the goals of social welfare, but these are the core of social work's function.

Social work has its function in common with every conscientious member of society. This has made its task especially difficult and still hampers its development as a separate profession. How can any endeavor be a profession when its end is simply the welfare of

[3] Unpublished letter to the author from Kyoko Kubota, August 12, 1955.

people? The answer can lie only in social work's recognition that this is true and that it, therefore, has to work closely with all private citizens who have accepted this task. It has no corner on a good conscience. As a profession its responsibility is to translate this conscience, this concern, into practical action. It must increase its sensitivity to the human problems in society and its knowledge of the forces that can prevent them. It must know the forces it can enlist to improve the conditions and the methods of enlisting them. These methods involve working with individuals, with groups, and with communities. Social work must know how to work with those who are deprived and with those who can help to avoid deprivation. If social workers become aware of this specific responsibility delegated to them they will not only be more humble in the knowledge of shared concern for human welfare, but they will also make a greater effort both to establish scientific facts and to clarify values to be achieved at a given time.

Much philosophical discussion in social work has taken the form of exhortation or accusation. One of the most frequent conflicts is between the "reformer" and the "individual therapist," and through the years the pendulum has swung constantly from one to the other. It would be easy to say that the social worker should be both: this simple answer involves the basic inquiry of this book, the relationship between science and ethics, between goals and means.

There have always been individuals in society who have been concerned because its services did not reach everyone. Some did this without considering theory or even the facts around them — they simply drove toward humane goals; sometimes they succeeded and sometimes they drifted so far away from reality that they were rightly called dreamers. Some developed theories without actively entering the struggle, yet very often "What they did was more decisive for history than many acts of statesmen who basked in brighter glory . . . it was this: they shaped and swayed men's minds." [4]

Social work is a *profession* that has as its specific goal the improvement of human society. It tries to use the ever-developing scientific

[4] Robert L. Heilbronner, *The Worldly Philosophers* (New York: Simon & Schuster, 1953), p. 3.

knowledge of forces within the individual and forces within society
to attain this goal. Social work is confronted not only with the
formulation of the theoretical system of values but with the testing
of this system in daily activities. This is an immense task and it is
therefore not surprising that confusion exists in this profession, that
at times it is praised by society and at times severely condemned,
that it shows insecurity and even the phenomenon of having practitioners who dislike their own identity as social workers. As a
profession, social work has assumed the age-old problem of the
relationship between the individual and society, of "facts infused
with values."

It will be the task of science to help social work more and more
with clarification of the facts. Philosophers should help with the
theoretical framework as a whole because, as Heilbronner said,
"Their common denominator is a common curiosity. They were all
fascinated by the world about them, its complexity and its seeming
disorder, by the cruelty which is so often masked in sanctimony and
the successes of which it was so often unaware. They were all absorbed in the behavior of their fellow man . . ." [5]

Social work has not produced great philosophers. As a profession
which is constantly called upon to solve urgent practical problems it
has had to use the thinking of others and concern itself mainly with
its methods. Out of this early concern with methods came the book
which marked social work's beginning as an independent profession,
Mary Richmond's *Social Diagnosis* (1917). Social work theory was
based on the humanities, but this fact was not always made clear.

One of the few social workers who consciously emphasized and
constantly reminded the profession of its philosophical base was
Eduard C. Lindeman. He came into social work before the field was
completely established and when teachers from many different
professions were accepted in its newly established schools. He came
into the profession by way of an interest in social issues and because
of a desire to put democratic ideas into practice. His early interest
was in recreation and community organization because they ex-

[5] *Ibid.*, p. 6.

pressed the freedom of independent voluntary groups and could be the means by which people learned to solve their own social problems. This interest soon led him into further consideration of the social group work method, which was focused especially on the participation of individuals in groups.

Soon after he began to teach he realized how closely related practical work with community problems was to the problems of social philosophy. He was deeply influenced by the educational philosophy of John Dewey. He was searching for answers to the questions of power and dependency, of the individual's freedom and his responsibility to the group, of helping people to be independent and yet to stand for specific solutions to social issues. The profession of social work — as pointed out in the previous examples — was and is constantly confronted with those problems of social philosophy. Lindeman devoted himself to the task of making social workers aware of this fact. In the early years of his association with the profession this attempt was well accepted. When, after World War I, the profession entered a period of more emphasis on clinical work with techniques especially designed for working with individuals, he was not as readily accepted. For this reason, he often turned his efforts outside the social work field — toward adult education, for instance. His contribution during this time was felt less among social workers because he was too far removed from their technical interests. Yet he kept alive a very important component of social work. It is significant that in the last years of his life the profession itself asked for more of his help with the problem of social philosophy. And he, in turn, became more interested in some of the methodology as well as in the dynamic understanding of the individual which had become an important part of social work.

Lindeman's contributions lay in his consistent determination never to separate human problems from philosophical consideration and in his demand that the profession not separate them.

This demand was effectively expressed in his classroom teaching and in the many lectures he gave all over the country. His writings, which expressed the same thoughts as his lectures, were not so effective because they lacked the personal impact of his dynamic and sincere personality. Yet they kept before social work continually the demand for a social philosophy.

Lindeman often stopped at the point of raising questions. He more often presented the stimulus for thought than thought itself, yet this stimulus was strong enough to influence students to accept philosophy as a vital component of their practice.

When a profession becomes more organized and its boundaries definite, the necessity for determining its philosophy becomes more urgent. Lindeman's contribution was considered important enough by his colleagues for them to establish a Lindeman Chair for the purpose of continuing the research into the relationship of social philosophy to social work. And, in the same spirit, the National Conference of Social Work established the Lindeman lectures to be presented at National Conferences of Social Welfare to preserve and renew the social philosophy perspective.

Because of Lindeman's importance, it seems justifiable to extract from his thinking his basic philosophy and the way he related it to the field of social work. This philosophy must be looked at in the framework of his time, but it is also necessary to determine what parts of it can be valuable for social work today. He would not want his ideas to be imposed dogmatically, but would welcome further developments of them.

It will therefore be part of this undertaking to add to Lindeman's thinking the knowledge we have gained through developing methods in social work in order to establish a philosophical framework for a profession which must maintain "the notion that a professional person lives in a world of both fact and value." [6]

While the emphasis here will be on the profession of social work, other professions and laymen too are clearly concerned with the same questions. Lindeman himself always pointed toward the partnership of the social work profession and the free citizen in a democratic society. Other professions and other disciplines can and should make additional contributions.

[6] Report by Lindeman, "The Place of Philosophy in the Curriculum of the New York School of Social Work: Past, Present and Future Considerations" (unpublished).

Such indeed is the true function of analysis in any category of research. Science dissects reality only in order to observe it better by virtue of a play of converging searchlights whose beams continually intermingle and inter-penetrate each other. Danger threatens only when each searchlight operator claims to see everything by himself, when each canton of learning pretends to national sovereignty.[7]

What follows is offered with humility and in the knowledge that I am only one searchlight operator. Others will see other facets of the profession and will emphasize other aspects of its philosophy and activities. The perspective of history and the various theories evolved by human beings about their own relationships have given insights to me, and the searching questions of students and colleagues from many parts of the world have stimulated me. I hope that this book will provide some answers — or at least that it will further in some way our never-ending quest to understand and to serve humanity.

[7] Marc Bloch, *The Historian's Craft* (New York: Knopf, 1953), p. 150.

PART ONE

Eduard C. Lindeman: The Man in His Time

"OUR eyes must be realistic and our feet realistic. We must walk in the right direction but we must walk step by step. Our tasks are: to define what is desirable; to carry out what is possible in the spirit of what is desirable." Salvador de Madariaga, quoted in Eduard C. Lindeman's notebook, 1944.

CHAPTER 1

THE FORMATIVE YEARS OF LINDEMAN'S LIFE

IN ORDER to understand a philosophical point of view we must first learn about the person who represents it, for philosophy grows out of the experiences, the thinking, the feelings — and out of the precious, intangible, unique part of man of which we understand so little. What follows will not be a detailed biography of Eduard C. Lindeman, but a short presentation of his life against the background of the time in which he lived and the profession in which he worked for most of his adult life.

All the friends, colleagues, and students of Lindeman whom I interviewed stressed the influence his personality had had on them, underlining the fact that he was not only a thinker but a human being with many interests and a great capacity for enjoying life. As his friend, Roger Baldwin, wrote in a memo in April 1955:

Ed was an idealist, and a very sensitive one, with his feet right on and in the earth. For all his idealism and his preoccupation with social thinking and action, he did not reject even the bawdy, nor a relaxed evening over drinks in some bar or beer hall, nor sports, games and dancing. And he loved the out-of-doors as I did, and like me, developed an absorbed interest in birdwatching.[1]

It is out of this wide interest in life that we must understand the man who saw social work in its broadest conception. His concern for people was immense. A colleague, Gordon Hamilton, said, "The most outstanding thing about him was his 'reverence for people.' "[2]

In a letter written by the poet Archibald MacLeish to Lindeman — probably in the 1930s — we find:

[1] Roger Baldwin, April 13, 1955.
[2] Gordon Hamilton, interview with the author, January 19, 1955.

I wish I had words to thank you for what you have done. But I must try. Not because you speak with generosity of the poem I have written but because you speak beautifully and with authority of the thing *I* tried to say. You so speak of it that it is now SAID. It was not before. I am grateful to you from the heart.[3]

CHILDHOOD AND YOUTH

Eduard C. Lindeman was born on May 9, 1885, in St. Claire, Michigan, one of ten children of immigrant parents who had come from Schleswig-Holstein, Denmark. His father, who worked in the salt mines of St. Claire, had escaped from a German prison and migrated to the United States after the Prussian-Danish War. As a young child, Lindeman was exposed to discrimination which he felt deeply. In a speech in 1945 he described this:

We lived in a neighborhood in which the Scandinavian people were held in low esteem; in fact, we were the lowest group in the community. Of all the immigrant groups, the Germans were the highest and the Scandinavians were the lowest. Thus I was born and brought up and spent my early childhood and youth in an environment in which if there was any segregation and demeaning of personality, they were practiced upon us; if there were any other names for children to be called, they were applied to us.[4]

These early influences and the background of his family were major causes of his fondness for Denmark, which he visited several times and from which he received impetus for his work in adult education. The family's language was German; Lindeman recalled that he had had difficulty in learning English and said that he had read Goethe and Schiller before he read Shakespeare. Yet the family had strong feelings against the German oppressor, and Lindeman quoted a motto found over the entrance of the first People's College (Folke Schule) in Denmark: "What the Prussians have taken from us by force without we must regain by education from within."[5]

His growing up as a member of a minority, torn by his allegiance

[3] Letter found in Lindeman's notebooks.
[4] Lindeman, "Palestine — Test of Democracy," *The Democratic Man*, Robert Gessner, ed. (Boston: Beacon Press, 1956), p. 249.
[5] "A Creative Opportunity for Libraries," unpublished paper read before the Southeastern Library Association, Asheville, N.C., 1924.

to several cultures, may explain the stress he put on "unity through diversity" and his continued struggle to understand group relations. Lindeman spoke little about his family, and perhaps he did not remember very much. The family was poverty-stricken, and suffered much from sickness and several accidental deaths. The father died when Eduard was nine, his mother a year later, leaving him in the care of his older sisters, Rose and Minnie. He remembered his father as a strict disciplinarian and a fundamentalist in religion, his mother as an intelligent soft-spoken woman who comforted him when he cried. In one of Lindeman's early articles we get a glimpse of his childhood delights and of the warmth of a large family.

I take my tree-friendships seriously, as indeed all friendships should be taken. In the yard of my old home stands a crooked chestnut tree. It is far from beautiful in shape, but to me it has a charm so intense that I renew its acquaintance as often as my business permits. Down its crooked trunk I slid from the window when they tried to keep me in bed with the mumps. Under its shade I started my first pin-store, and with its fruit I've won many a battle. I cannot estimate the value of that tree in dollars, but I do know that if it were to become diseased, I would consider it my duty to give it aid. To go back to the old home and find the chestnut tree missing would be like finding a forever-empty chair at the family table.[6]

After a few years in grammar school, Lindeman worked as a riveter in the shipyards, as a farm laborer, and in the salt mines. We know little of how he became interested in books and learning; he may have been influenced by an older brother who, he mentions, liked reading. A poem, "The Day Is Best," written in his early twenties before he started his formal training, shows an abundance of enjoyment of life and a real feeling for language.

> Were I to make my choice of time of day,
> 'Twould be a task for me to say,
> Just what is best.

> At break of morn when I a'laboring go
> New life in my whole being seems aglow,
> For I've had rest.

[6] Lindeman, "Save the Grand Old Trees," *The Gleaner*, Vol. XVIII, No. 12, September 1915, p. 6.

> When midday is reached and toiling muscles tire,
> I still rejoice because my tasks require
> A daily test.
>
> And now, at dusk, when lowering shadows fall,
> My heart leaps higher at the homeward call
> And all is blessed.[7]

However and whenever he acquired it, his urge for learning was exceedingly strong. His first step toward formal education came about when a farmer for whom he was working read that students could enter Michigan State without a high school diploma if they could prove that they were able to undertake the studies. The farmer gave his well-read helper this information. Lindeman saved $74 out of his wages and in 1906 applied for entrance.

His poor command of English almost barred him from Michigan State — at that time an agricultural college also offering courses in science, sociology, psychology, and the like — but a woman professor took an interest and tutored him privately in the language. His life was further complicated when his money was stolen and he almost had to leave college.

In his first published book Lindeman described a time in his senior year when he felt forced to discontinue his studies.

I was riding to the city one day, when I felt a touch on my shoulder. It was the Secretary's wife. She gently asked me if it were true that I had planned to leave college. I told her about my financial trouble. In her big-hearted, kindly way she replied, "You won't have to leave school; you go and see the Secretary. He wants to talk with you." I called on the Secretary a few days later. He told me that he was not going to permit me to leave college at this time, when the goal was so near, on account of a little financial difficulty.[8]

The college secretary helped him find work on the campus which financed the rest of his studies. He took care of thirty cows and several hundred fowl before breakfast and did some landscape gardening over the weekends and on vacations. His working capacity — as later in life — was enormous.

[7] Lindeman, *College Characters: Essays and Verse* (Port Huron, Mich.: Riverside Printing Co., 1911).
[8] *Ibid.*, pp. 30–32.

He soon triumphed over the language handicap with which he had entered college and became an outstanding student in spite of his heavy workload. He was president of the campus YMCA; he worked on the college paper, *The Holcad*, editing it for two years; he wrote and directed a play, "In the Hearts of the People," which was produced on the campus in 1909; and he became the manager of the college football team. In 1911 he graduated with high honor.

Going to college and reading books gave him an opportunity to re-think and strengthen the ideas he had formed during his life as a laborer. He found an outlet for his ideas — which were then largely socialist — in the college YMCA. At that time there was a conflict in the YMCA movement between the conservative element and the faction represented by Walter Rauschenbusch, a Christian Socialist.[9] Another influence on the YMCA movement — and thus on Lindeman — came through the Federal Council of Churches of Christ in America; this organization encouraged the participation of laymen in church affairs and advocated a practical revival of Christian principles. Although the YMCA did not adopt the "Social Creed of the Churches" sponsored by the Council until 1919, many leaders had long been actively promoting it.[10]

Further excerpts from Lindeman's *College Characters* reveal his developing views on various subjects. He insisted that students must take a stand on politics and that this was important for everybody. Yet he was able to accept other opinions, for instance that of the conservative secretary of the college: "I am glad that the secretary's viewpoint is different." At another place in the same volume he says that we should "love people in spite of wide differences of opinion." Or, "The law of nature is variety in unity and unity in variety. Unity without variety is dead uniformity. . . ."

In addition to the principle of "variety in unity" in this early writing, there are two other ideas expressed which Lindeman con-

[9] Walter Rauschenbusch was a clergyman who argued that capitalism was the most formidable enemy to the Kingdom of God. In 1907 he published his major book, *Christianity and the Social Crisis*, which indicted capitalism as anti-Christian.

[10] C. Howard Hopkins, *History of the YMCA in North America* (New York: New York Association Press, 1951), pp. 528–29.

tinued to develop all his life: first, the application of ethical principles to practice, and second, the attempt to unify science and religion. The first is expressed in a discussion of the race problem: "The great problem that confronts the American People today is a national problem; it hinges upon whether or not this great nation of ours is great enough to live up to its own convictions, carry out its own declaration of independence, and execute the provisions of its own constitution. We need less theology, less legislation, and more brotherhood; less declamation and more common sense."

The second principle is expressed in a short essay, "Science and Religion." He regarded the battle between Darwinism and religion as finished. His way of proving that science and religion can be reconciled was quite naive. Reading the essay, one realizes that young Lindeman was struggling to persuade himself: he was striving for a "religion without prejudice and faith in science."

In this little volume we also get a glimpse into the personality of the young man — his loneliness, his yearning for a family, his desperate search for a philosophy, and the comfort he got from his closeness to nature. He very much appreciated an invitation from the secretary of the college: "To one who had so long been without the comforts of a true home . . ." And there is a desperate cry in a poem titled "What I Ask of Friendship."

> I do not ask that friends shall share with me of
> worldly goods;
> I do not ask that friends shall bear with me in
> sundry moods;
> I only ask, as long as I walk straight and do the
> right —
> I only ask that they believe me honest in my
> fight.

This cry for friendship and his wish that at least his motives should not be questioned were characteristic of him all through his life. His later friends spoke of his great sincerity and his unhappiness when others questioned his motivation. He never feared disagreement but he did fear malice. Oddly enough his loneliness was probably increased by his urgent drive to better understand human relations and the purpose of life. In "The Cycle," a class poem written for graduation in 1911, he said, "But he in quest must flaunt the face of care." And in another poem,

> Great God where canst Thou be?
> I ever search for Thee
> In all mine eyes behold;
> And Thou doest yet withhold
> From me Thy tender hand.
> How can I understand?

Written by a twenty-six-year-old man who had not lived a sheltered youth, this indicates real conflict and unhappiness.

Nature was his greatest helper. "My greatest battles have been fought . . . alone and in the quiet of Nature's charm. After all, we settle very few questions by argument. Our greatest convictions come to us in solitude." [11]

Yet he also loved people. It was during his college days that he met his wife-to-be. The dean of women had invited him to a Christmas party for students who had no homes to go to during the holidays; she also invited some girls from the college, among them Hazel Taft, the daughter of Levi Rawson Taft, professor of horticulture and landscape gardening. Member of a conservative old American family that was related to William Howard Taft, she was a very young student, having entered college at sixteen.

Shortly after the party at which they met, she heard Lindeman speak at a mass meeting he had called in behalf of a student who had been unjustly dismissed. She recalls that his protests were so strong and convincing that the student was reinstated. She was impressed; she felt that he "made sense"; they began to see each other often. He was soon welcome in the Taft household, although at first the father considered him a radical and opposed the friendship.

Lindeman and Hazel Taft were married in August 1912, a year after his graduation.

BEGINNINGS OF A CAREER

During his college years Lindeman became interested in the cooperative movement which was gaining strength in Michigan. Grant

[11] Lindeman, *op. cit.*, pp. 32, 52, 104, 105, 68, 35, 111, 128, 143, 21.

Slocum, managing editor of a fighting farm newspaper published in Detroit, the *Gleaner*, advocated cooperatives and stood for the interests of small farmers who were harassed by the "middlemen." The *Gleaner* had initiated one of the first insurance plans for farmers, and it took up other everyday rural problems. It fought to get cheaper twine for them and to induce the United States Post Office to deliver parcels to their homes instead of forcing the farmers to pick up parcels at central places or pay high freights to private trucking companies. Slocum was a firebrand, interested in young people and their advancement. We do not know how he became acquainted with Eduard Lindeman,[12] but in October 1911 Lindeman was introduced to the readers as the new managing editor of the *Gleaner*.

We are greatly pleased this month to introduce Edward C. Lindemann, who has accepted the position of Managing Editor of this publication. Mr. Lindemann not only comes to us well qualified for this very important position through his college training, but brings the energy, enthusiasm and interest so necessary in successfully carrying forward the *Gleaner's* progressive policies in the interest of better farms, better farming and better business farmers. . . . While a student he was a member of the first class in agricultural journalism and edited its first publication. He was also editor in chief of the college weekly and President of the Young Men's Christian Association. He was offered the Managing Editorship soon after completing his course; but so many avenues were open to him, that it was not until after an intense personal struggle as to the proper sphere in which to devote his energies, that he decided to throw his life in the interest of the farmer. This young man is a deep thinker, a logical reasoner and intensely interested in agriculture and rural problems. He believes that there is a bright future for the American farmer; believes in the cooperative methods for which *The Gleaner* has so conscientiously fought, and with these convictions in mind and an earnest desire to see the farmer come into his own, he considers *The Gleaner* the best opportunity for the opening up of his life's work.[13]

[12] Miss Mabel Claire Ladd, librarian of the *Gleaner* who has been with it since its beginning, thinks that Slocum had hired Lindeman to do landscape gardening during his college days, and also that Slocum probably received high recommendations from the college about Lindeman.

[13] Grant Slocum, *The Gleaner*, Vol. XVII, No. 1, October 1911, p. 3. Lindeman's name is spelled with two n's during his time with the *Gleaner*. It is possible that he changed the spelling later.

The articles under Lindeman's name suggest some of his lifelong interests.

His concern about soil and forest conservation is apparent in "Save the Grand Old Trees."

I watched the workmen fell a giant white pine, and as that majestic old tree fell to the ground, I felt something in its moan. It was more than a century in the making, but a few minutes of man's labor ended its career. And so, we have gone on devastating our land of its forests, leaving the barren land open to the ravages of the floods.[14]

His desire to protect those who are "dependent," in this case the small truck farmers, is shown in another article.

Many people, especially city people, have been enticed to invest in Michigan fruit lands. The land of all sections has been highly advertised for its exceptional qualifications for fruit-growing. In this manner many have been deceived into buying the very poorest land in the state under the impression that they were to become wealthy through fruit-growing. These misrepresentations are a blight upon our state. The writer wishes to state clearly that there is much poor land in northern Michigan. . . . All who invest in property should be careful to determine its true qualifications. If such knowledge is not in the possession of the investor, he should consult an expert who will give an honest opinion. There has been altogether too much dishonesty connected with Michigan fruit and Michigan land.[15]

The beginnings of his advocacy of the principle of cooperation and of his insistence on citizens' participating in public affairs are apparent in a 1912 article.

From January 9th to the 12th fifteen hundred Gleaners — the largest gathering of real farmers ever called together — met at South Bend, Indiana, for the purpose of discussing the business of their organization. The keynote of the whole convention was "Cooperation." The delegates were unanimous in declaring the farmers' cooperation in the marketing of crops. These delegates represented nearly 90,000 farmers of the middle west. They have gone back to their respective communities to fight for cooperation. What will be the result? Mr. Grant Slocum believes that the farmers of this section will own enough elevators and shipping stations to control the market within

[14] *The Gleaner*, Vol. XVIII, No. 12, September 1912, p. 6.
[15] "A Venture in Fruit Growing Farther North," *The Gleaner*, Vol. XVII, No. 2, November 1911, p. 6.

the next five years. What do you believe, and what are you going to do in order to make your belief come true? [16]

In December 1911, "Education for Busy Farmers" appeared; it described short courses in agricultural education at Michigan Agricultural College and urged farmers to take advantage of them.[17] It was not outstanding in content, but this article demonstrated an interest in adult education that had not appeared in the *Gleaner* before.

The *Gleaner*'s principles were based on a combination of Christian and democratic philosophies, which coincided with Lindeman's thinking at this time. In 1912 the magazine published a declaration of principles which showed this combination.

We, the duly authorized representatives of *The Gleaner* organization, in convention assembled, believing that the aims and objects of the Order are not fully understood, hereby set forth the following declaration of principles, as intimately bearing upon the life of the American Farmer.

FIRST. A religion so broad and elevating in its character as to be a worthy parent of that spirit of fraternity advocated and practiced by this Society, as well as to develop the elements of civic righteousness, individual intelligence, and a high order of citizenship that shall have a lasting effect upon our entire national life, and which shall lead the individual to that higher plane as exemplified in the daily life and teachings of the lowly Nazarene.

SECOND. So broad a conception of our political responsibilities that we shall rise above the contaminating atmosphere of partisanship, and exercise our right of suffrage for men and principles unhampered by bigotry and ignorance. We believe that the farmer should have a voice in formulating the laws under which he lives in proportion to his national commercial importance, and believing that all laws, both state and national, should emanate from the people, and that they should directly control the official conduct and acts of our public servants, as well as have the right to repeal such laws now existing as are a menace to our national well-being, we favor the initiative, referendum and re-call, and further favor the

[16] Lindeman, "Cooperation Is the Next Step," *The Gleaner*, Vol. XVIII, No. 5, February 1912, p. 6.

[17] *The Gleaner*, Vol. XVIII, No. 3, December 1911. This article does not carry Lindeman's byline, but Miss Ladd, the librarian, is quite sure that Lindeman wrote it; moreover, the style is his.

election of the President of the United States and United States senators by a direct vote.[18]

Combined with this interest in political issues was work with the local charities. The *Gleaner* started a movement to bring city children into the country for their vacations. In a 1911 article, "Give Fresh Air to the City Children," it called on farmers to take city youngsters into their homes. Typical of the mood of the time was the insistence on the fact that the children were "poor but clean little tots." [19]

Though Lindeman continued all his life to be interested in writing, journalism did not seem to satisfy him. Apparently he wanted to do more direct practical work as well as to write. His first move toward practical social work came in 1913 when he became assistant to the pastor of Plymouth Congregational Church in Lansing, working with the church-sponsored boys' club. The next step was a position he took in 1914 at the Michigan Agricultural College as extension worker responsible for the program of the state boys' and girls' clubs — forerunners of today's 4H clubs. He was active in the American Recreation Association, and took part in its congress at Grand Rapids in 1916. In 1917 he participated in the War Camp Community Service, which offered recreational services to soldiers.

In 1918 the family moved from Michigan and Lindeman started teaching at the YMCA College in Chicago. He stayed there for only a short time — not quite a year. He was dissatisfied with the conservatism in the college and felt he "could not take it." During this time he met Jane Addams of Hull House, and was a member of one of the first groups of social workers to take a short course at Hull House.

Lindeman's concern for community action was great. He wanted to understand better how one could help communities determine their own fate and how experts and citizens could work together. Out of this concern grew *The Community*, published in 1921. It was written in Greensboro but based on his experience in Michigan. This is clearly expressed in his dedication:

[18] "Declaration of Principles," *The Gleaner*, Vol. XVIII, No. 5, February 1912, p. 6.
[19] *The Gleaner*, Vol. XVI, No. 9, June 1911, p. 9.

*To the communities of the State of Michigan — Towns, Villages,
and Open Country — and Their Leaders with Whom I was Privileged to Spend Four Happy Years of Intimate Service, and from
Whom I Learned Most of What I Have Here Presented Concerning
The Community.*[20]

INTEREST IN COMMUNITY AND GROUP PROCESS

The Community aroused a great deal of interest. One of those
who read it with special attention was Mary Parker Follett, who
shared Lindeman's interest in community action. They began to
correspond, and eventually she met him. She was a brilliant young
woman, a lecturer and writer on civic issues whose major interests
were vocational guidance and civic education. During the war years
she had worked in community centers in the United States and later
she free-lanced, writing and lecturing. When she met Lindeman she
was working on a major book, *Creative Experience*, published in
1924, and she was already known for *The New State, Group Organization. The Solution of Popular Government*, published in 1918.
In it she put great emphasis on creative social experience. The crucial concepts presented in *The New State* were the following: (1)
Social experience is the basis of state structure. (2) Sovereignty is
relative to the capacity to rule oneself, to rule a group or a state.
(3) State structure is the expression of elements of identity in purpose. (4) The will of a group is not atomic but is the common
expression of individual wills. (5) Rich experience can only come
through actual experiences in group life. There must be experience
in a variety of groups. Because of the multiplicity of human nature
no one group can exhaust the capacity of the modern citizen. (6) Individual and group are not antitheses. (7) The individual is the
ultimate unit which is more diversified than any group can be. (8)
There is no necessary contradiction between the citizen and the
state. (9) Freedom and determinism are not opposites. (10) Self
and others are not opposites.

As practical consequences of her theory she saw the necessity for
citizenship training through free group association and for intensive

[20] Lindeman, *The Community* (New York: Association Press, 1921).

adult and worker's education. She considered neighborhood education one of the most important and pressing problems in 1918.

Mary Follett's thinking about individuals in relation to groups was far ahead of her time. She distinguished clearly among crowd, mob, and group. She described how experts could work with committees to help leadership emerge. She realized the dual aspect of the group, that it was a union of individuals but it also presented an individual in a larger union. She insisted that the reform movement had been wrong in not using the group process. "The group process must be learned by practice." What must be taught, she believed, was interdependence and discipline in building a whole of which the individual was a part. To her the schools and community centers were the true universities of a democracy. Individuals who had difficulties in society could be helped through group work.

In *The New State* she wrote of group work for delinquent children and described Thomas Mott Osborne's attempts at Sing Sing to use group relations to prepare offenders for community life. Her basic philosophy and her understanding of the individual's relation to the group remains valid today, as is evident in the quotations that follow.

Now that we know that there is no such thing as a separate ego, that individuals are created by reciprocal interplay, our whole study of psychology is being transformed.

[The group process is] an acting and reacting, a single and identical process which brings out differences and integrates them into a unity.

Unity, not conformity, must be our aim. We attain unity only through variety.

Democracy is the rule of an interacting, interpermeating whole. . . . is faith in humanity, not faith in "poor" people or "ignorant" people, but faith in every living soul.

The great cosmic force in the womb of humanity is latent in the group as its creative energy; that it may appear the individual must do his duty every moment. We do not get the whole power of the group unless every individual is given full value, is giving full value.

Never settle down within the theory you have chosen, the cause you have embraced; know that another theory, another cause exist and seek that. The enhancement of life is not for the comfort-lover. As soon as you succeed — real success means something arising to overthrow your security.[21]

In addition to being valid for present-day social work as well as for her own time, these excerpts show parallels between Mary Parker Follett's and Lindeman's thinking. In *The Community* Lindeman had discussed and asked for intelligent group action. He had also pointed out the important relationship between the individual and his group. The principle of "unity through diversity" had been expressed in his early book, *College Characters*.

In the introduction to *Creative Experience*, Mary Follett described her relationship to Lindeman:

With Professor Eduard C. Lindeman my work has been still more closely connected. For two years Mr. Lindeman has engaged in a study of marketing cooperatives not only for the purpose of investigating an aspect of the cooperative movement, but also in order to observe an acute form of social conflict, that between farmers and middlemen. Mr. Lindeman and I shared the hope that from this investigation certain conclusions might be drawn which would be valuable for social conflict in general, and also that there might be developed some fruitful methods of social research in line with the general advance in sociological thinking. In recognition of much that was common in our aims, we decided that it would be advantageous to maintain a rather close working connection, and we have therefore had conferences from time to time from which I have learned as freely as I wished, material which shows great discernment and more subtle and intangible workings that often reveal the real values of a situation. I have used certain illustrations which he has given me and others which I have gained from going over a large amount of printed matter (cooperative news organs, propagandist pamphlets, contract forms, contested cases, etc.) which he has sent me. Mr. Lindeman's own forthcoming book *Social Discovery, An Approach to the Study of Functional Groups*, seems to me a valuable contribution toward that new technique of social research which is so badly needed today.[22]

[21] Mary Parker Follett, *The New State* (New York: Longmans, 1934), 4th ed., pp. 334, 19, 33, 156, 39, 342.
[22] Mary Parker Follett, *Creative Experience* (New York: Longmans, 1924), pp. xviii–xix. Lindeman's *Social Discovery* was published in 1924.

NEW INFLUENCES

In 1919 — a family man with four small daughters — he was called to Greensboro, North Carolina, as director of the sociology department of the North Carolina College for Women. Almost from the first, he had difficulty fitting into the conservatism of a southern community. In a letter to Mrs. William A. McGraw, written during his first year in Greensboro, he told of a faculty meeting at which a group of faculty members wanted to dictate teaching methods. His opening comments were, "On an occasion like this one is tempted to say those things which are pleasing and soothing rather than those which ring true to the inner conscience. With God's help I shall not yield to that temptation this morning." These words, rather pompous and heavy for such an occasion, show Lindeman's discomfort when he had to contradict colleagues. In the same letter he described a discussion with his class on the question of what an industrial YMCA should do in case of a strike. "You would have been amused at the timid, shilly-shallying, straddle-the-fence attitude which the class wanted to take. You may be sure that I did not permit them to be comfortable in this attitude. . . ." [23]

When, in addition to this rather unorthodox teaching, his family also did not make enough distinction between the Negroes and themselves to suit some of the townspeople, the Ku Klux Klan, then in its heyday, went into action. The newspapers began to attack him and his family, distorted facts were spread, and Lindeman decided it would be best to leave. Although he was in the employ of the college until 1921, he interrupted his stay with a trip to Denmark, where he studied adult education and cooperatives — two aspects of Danish life which impressed him profoundly and influenced his thinking a great deal.

In April 1920, in his capacity as chairman of the Committee on Recreation and Sociable Life of the American Country Life Association in Greensboro, he gave his first paper before the National Conference of Social Work, held that year in New Orleans. His topic was "Organization and Technique for Rural Recreation." The

[23] Quoted in *The Democratic Man*, Robert Gessner, ed. (Boston: The Beacon Press, 1956), pp. 126, 127.

speech was full of his preoccupation with the principles of community organization and his wish to combine psychological and sociological viewpoints. He wanted, he said, to work out a technique for rural social work — to get away from a trial-and-error method and make greater use of scientific facts. This is particularly significant because during the same period a similar attempt was being made in the field of social casework by Mary Richmond. The fact that Mary Richmond and Lindeman did not know of each other shows the vastness and the segmentation of social work — and also shows that at that stage in the development of social work various areas of practice were completely unrelated.

Realizing how impossible Lindeman's position in Greensboro had become, Mary Follett introduced him to Herbert Croly and Dorothy Whitney Straight, both of whom were connected with the *New Republic*. As a result of this meeting, Mrs. Straight helped to finance Lindeman so that he could do free-lance writing and private research from 1922 to 1924.

He and his family moved to High Bridge, New Jersey, into a house that must have meant much to a man who felt so close to the land. It was a large house on top of a hill, surrounded by thirty-four acres of woods. A small part of this area was rented to a nearby farmer. Recalling this time, one of Lindeman's daughters writes:

Our home was called Greystone and we all loved it — including our beautiful Seeing-Eye dog, Lasca, which we acquired from Dad's friend . . . We did not farm, although we had a nice orchard, a wonderful vegetable garden filled with corn in August and all sorts of vegetables and a lovely flower garden. Dad's favorite pastime, when not working upstairs in his third floor study, was puttering around in the rock garden, where he had accumulated, from various sources, some rather rare and precious plants. He later built a tennis court which gave my parents — and the community — many pleasurable hours. . . . He spent many a happy hour both building and keeping and playing on this tennis court. . . . Dad particularly loved the big tall spruce trees and was very sad when Mrs. Taylor, the former owner, proceeded later on to take some of them away. He taught us to garden — taught us about nature in general — helped us to start a little local paper with news of goings-on at Greystone.

These two years of private research were probably the easiest ones for the family. Those were years when Lindeman was at home more, studying and writing. It was not long before the demands made on him by other activities took him away from the family a great deal. His daughter continues:

However, much of our life at Greystone was without Dad — he was coming and going most of the time it seemed. The familiar old battered suitcase and briefcase seemed to be forever sitting in the hall waiting to be unpacked or ready to go again. The excitement when we all rushed down to the station to meet the 6:30 P.M. train was terrific and even more so the moment when he would open up his bag and give us each some thoughtful present — when at home he read aloud to us in the evenings a great deal — he loved American humor stories — and he was patient about watching our feeble attempt to put on plays and dances for him. He was encouraging whenever we tried to write stories or poems, play an instrument, paint or sculpt.[24]

The two years of private research were filled with writing and new and exciting contacts with two significant groups: the people associated with the *New Republic* — Herbert Croly, its editor, and Walter Lippmann, its associate editor and columnist for the *New York World*; and the Inquiry group, including Robert MacIver and John Dewey, who were both teaching at Columbia at the time.

The Inquiry, originally named the National Conference on the Christian Way of Life, was concerned with problems of religious education and social ethics. It had been created by a resolution of the administrative committee of the Federal Council of the Churches of Christ in America in 1922. This resolution asked for an inquiry into "The Meaning of Christianity for Human Relationships, with special attention to industry, citizenship and race relations in the United States and the function of the church in social and civic affairs." The Federal Council gave utmost freedom to the conference. It did not assume responsibility for its promotion. The conference had realized that many organizations worked on this but had developed different solutions. It was concerned because many people were members of organizations but did not participate. "Sensitive people have become

[24] Letter from Mrs. George Leonard to the author, January 19, 1956.

as dissatisfied with a mere repetition of general ethical formulas, which, seemingly, no large group of professed Christians were seriously trying to apply — and which perhaps could not be practically applied — as they were with the panaceas so sedulously offered by one-sided propagandists." The members of the Inquiry tried to use newer methods, "a method that would endeavor to embody the lessons of the more recent experience in adult education and in the adjustment of group conflict."

Committees formed under the auspices of the Inquiry consisted of people from all walks of life. Deciding to take a realistic approach to concrete problems, they started with the question of international relations, but were not afraid to tackle even more controversial questions — for instance, the role of the church in the community. In their publication they rarely cited names of people who participated: "It does not rely on the powers of some single outstanding personality: It has no regular membership: Its only financial resources are the voluntary contributions of individual participants. It is not an agency or a movement, but just an 'organized move.'" In this material we find many references to social work and its problems during this postwar period. One of the publications says: "Social workers watch with dismay the loss of spiritual dynamics in movements for human betterment at a time of unequaled progress in the movement of technique." [25]

The meetings of the Inquiry group continued until 1929 and had a strong influence on Lindeman. At this time he fully accepted Dewey's pragmatism and became interested in research of group process and group participation.

In 1922 Lindeman spoke at a Recreation Congress. In the audience was Walter Pettit, faculty member of the New York School of Social Work. He caught Lindeman's contagious feeling for people and his capacity to apply psychological and value theories to practice.

[25] All this information is taken from Bruno Lasker, ed., *Information Service*, Vol. IV, No. 11, March 14, 1925, published by the Department of Research and Education, Christianity and Human Relations, Federal Council of Churches of Christ in America.

After listening to Lindeman, Walter Pettit returned to New York and urged the director of the School, Porter Lee, to ask Eduard C. Lindeman to become a member of the faculty. Dorothy Straight, who was one of the trustees of the New York School, helped to persuade him to accept.

CHAPTER 2

TEACHER AT THE NEW YORK SCHOOL
OF SOCIAL WORK

IN ORDER to understand Lindeman's position in a school of social work one must examine the development of such schools and of the profession. The years following World War I were the period when social work was consolidated as a profession with a specific body of knowledge and skills that differentiated it from other professions; this consolidation had begun in the early years of the century, but it was accelerated in the postwar years.

Social workers were especially concerned at this time with casework, a concern that can be related to several factors. First, there were general and far-reaching social changes which involved human emotions: revolutions in Russia and Germany, the emancipation of women, and the rising importance of labor. And secondly, the mental hygiene movement developed rapidly and psychiatric knowledge was used more and more in treatment. During World War I it became apparent that many breakdowns were not exclusively physical, and psychiatric services were established on a larger scale. The social work profession tried to understand those social changes better, to learn more about the theories of human behavior, and to educate practitioners to use this knowledge systematically.

From 1900 to 1905, courses or schools for social workers had sprung up in several parts of the country. During the twenties they began to consolidate. For instance, in 1904 the extension division of the University of Chicago had established an institute of social science which developed into an independent School of Civics and Philanthropy. In 1920 this school was incorporated into the graduate school of Social Service Administration. Edith Abbott gives an interesting description of the thinking which led to this decision.

We had had discussions over a long period of time with the University of Chicago about the possible transfer of the work of the school. We were very insistent, however, upon one point. We said that the School would give up its work as an independent institution and move to the University only if the University would give the school the status of a graduate professional school that was enjoyed by a law school. We were not willing to become a part of any social science department, nor were we willing to be just another department in a graduate school of arts, literature and science. It was clear to us that professional education for our field would make necessary the use of courses given in several different university departments, and we were not willing to be submerged in any one of them. More important, however, was the fact that we needed a new kind of program including class work, field work and research in our special field, and this kind of professional program could not develop in any one of the social science departments.[1]

Common planning among the various schools of social work started in May 1919, when an informal conference in which fifteen schools participated was called in New York. Among the resolutions passed at this conference were three directly related to common curriculum content:

That at some stage in the training of professional social workers, before the award of a certificate or a degree, there be included instructions in Economics, Biology, Sociology, Psychology and Political Science.

That it is desirable that the professional training of all social workers should include technical courses in casework, statistics and some form of community work.

That it is desirable that the professional training of all social workers should include courses in labor problems, health and social legislation.

[1] Edith Abbott, "Twenty-One Years of Education for the Social Services," *Social Service Review*, XV, December 1941, pp. 671–72. Miss Abbott was born in 1876. Her father was at one time lieutenant governor of Nebraska. After she took her Ph.D. in economics in 1905 from the University of Chicago, she went to the London School of Economics. Influenced by the social theories of the Webbs, she returned to Chicago to become head resident of Hull House and member of the faculty of the school in 1913. From 1924 on she was dean of the school.

One which suggested a closer association:

That a committee of five be appointed to prepare a form of organization for a future Association of Training Schools.[2]

The Association of Training Schools for Professional Social Workers was constituted on June 4, 1919, in Atlantic City, its purpose "to develop standards of training for professional social work." The constitution provided that "Any educational institution maintaining a full-time course of training for professional social work covering at least one academic year and including a substantial amount of both class instruction and of supervised field work, may become a member of the Association upon election by the Executive Committee." [3]

The strongest focus of the schools was on the new knowledge about the individual. The rapidly changing social scene also produced many new organizations concerned with ideologies, cultural emphasis, social reconstruction, and intergroup relations. Until about 1910, the great reform movements had been concerned with economic deprivation and with ignorance among poor and exploited new immigrants. The prime movers of such reform were idealists from outside the underprivileged group, working in its behalf.

In the years during and shortly after World War I, the tenor of the times was revolutionary, with a heavy emphasis on voluntary associations which could provide self-help. Reform moved more into the hands of those who needed it. Youth agencies for *all* young people were founded. Community centers with greater emphasis on self-government sprang up.

In contrast to Europe, the United States has known practically no political youth organizations but the emphasis of both the community and the youth organizations was on the democratic ideals of the Constitution and related to the newly found freedom for women. It was this swing toward democratic independent organizations that made up another aspect of social work at this time. Ideas about group work were not yet part of the material taught in schools of

[2] Typewritten minutes of the conference (Library, New York School of Social Work).

[3] Typewritten minutes (Library, New York School of Social Work).

social work, but they were alive and presented at national conferences.

It was on this wing that Eduard C. Lindeman moved into the social work profession. His concern was with rural youth, with the independent self-help organizations of farmers, and with recreation as the time in an individual's life when he is free from the burden of daily labor and can be active as a citizen. This area of concern had not yet developed a theory, had not been related much to the psychological insights of casework, and had not yet developed a diagnostic approach. It was a fringe area of social work, but it had powerful possibilities.

In 1924 Lindeman joined the faculty of the New York School of Social Work. His interests at that time are best expressed in his unpublished manuscript, "The Place of Philosophy in the Curriculum of the New York School of Social Work."

When I first came to the New York School of Social Work it was assumed that my major interest was in the field of Community Organization. My first published work was in this field (THE COMMUNITY — 1921). During the first decade of my employment there was a tacit understanding between myself and Director Porter Lee that I was to continue my outside interest and hence my salary at the school was for a long time kept at a figure lower than that of other full-time teachers. Among the interests which occupied my attention outside the School were four which exercised a determining influence upon me and in turn upon my teaching at the School. These interests were:

a. *The Inquiry*: an examination into the Christian way of life which gradually was transmuted into the Democratic Way of Life. Among the persons with whom I worked in this association were: E. C. Carter, Dwight Sheffield, Bruno Lasker, Rhoda McCullough, John Hader and Robert MacIver. The general cast of thought of this group was philosophic; in fact, the two chief influences which motivated this group were John Dewey and Mary Follett.

b. *The New School for Social Research* with which I became associated at this time and where I was brought into contact with John Dewey, Charles Beard, James Harvey Robinson, Thorstein Veblen, Wesley Mitchell, Alvin Johnson, Dr. Adler and others who represented a critical attitude towards conventional or academic scholarship. The major thread of conviction in this group was in the direction of synthesis of subject-matter, particularly of the social sciences, and it will thus be seen that I was again subjected to what was in reality a philosophic trend of thought.

c. *The New Republic*, which was then under the guidance of its founder, Herbert Croly, and to which I became attached as contributing editor. The men with whom I here came into working relations were, in addition to Croly, Walter Lippmann, Walter Weyl, George Soule, Edmund Wilson, Malcolm Cowley, Charles Merz, Francis Hackett, Stark Young, et cetera, and here again I found myself in the company of men who were engaged in criticism and whose principal tools were philosophic. Herbert Croly, who was probably the chief influence of my life at this period, was himself a first-rate philosopher and his *Promise of American Life* was my first introduction to the notion that cultural interpretation might become primarily a philosophic enterprise.

d. *Mary Follett* spent some time visiting me in Greensboro, North Carolina, that is, previous to my coming to New York and we agreed upon a collaboration. It finally turned out that we wrote separate books (*Creative Experience*, M. F., and *Social Discovery*, E. C. L.) but our long association had a profound effect upon my thought. She was at that time, emerging from her earlier Hegelian period, and although I did not think of myself as a philosopher, I was devoting more and more time to reading in philosophy and had come under John Dewey's influence, which experience led me away from whatever remnants of absolution remained in my make-up. My arguments with Miss Follett persuaded me that I had gradually become a pragmatist, and it was at this juncture that I reached the conviction that the social sciences needed supplementation from philosophy, especially that branch of philosophy which was then striving to align itself with scientific method, namely, American pragmatism or Instrumentalism.

The above synoptic sketch describes how my thought was being influenced at the very time that I was beginning my teaching career at the New York School. The four influences sketched above were so powerful that philosophy crept into my teaching almost imperceptibly and without clear recognition on my part. In other words, I began inserting philosophy into my courses without awareness that I was gradually moving away from technical concerns and in the direction of values and principles.[4]

Lindeman entered the teaching of social work at a time when the

[4] Lindeman, "The Place of Philosophy in the Curriculum of the New York School of Social Work: Past, Present and Future Considerations," 1950 (typewritten), pp. 1–3.

forces in social work were struggling to determine the content of its professional education. This effort is not yet ended, but it was especially vivid at this time. The New York School of Social Work had been the first in the country to offer professional education and had developed through changing opinions in regard to curriculum.[5] The first definite decision about the direction the School would follow had come in 1917 after two of the School's leaders, Edward T. Devine and Samuel McCune Lindsay, fought out their differences. Both were interested in reform; but Lindsay wanted to put more emphasis on academic work, while Devine placed greater emphasis upon practical experience. It was Devine who won out.

From Lindeman's attempted interpretative history of the School we gain a great deal of insight into his view of its early struggles.

During the second decade of the Twentieth Century it became clear that two new and to some extent antithetical forces were exercising a dominant influence upon social thought. On the one hand, the impact of the "new" psychology had precipitated discussions which actually brought about a shift in causal reasoning: whereas it had become customary during the Darwinian and the Spencerian periods of the Nineteenth Century to attribute social disorganization to environmental causes it now became increasingly apparent that some of the causes of personal maladjustment were to be found in the "inner" life of individuals. So-called Freudian psychology had "arrived" and was beginning to penetrate the various professions dealing with human behavior. The new school of social work in New York City was soon to feel the impact of this movement in thought.

At the same time it was also becoming clear that modern industrial societies were creating another human need which was destined to exert a determining influence upon the new profession of social work. Industrial societies were exhibiting a paradoxical outcome: increased industrialization appeared to produce increased insecurity among workers. The demand for security which was thus engendered gave rise to that new force in politics which now goes by the name of the Welfare State.

Of these two new forces, the one which was to give coloration to the profession of social work through the New York School of Social

[5] The New York Charity Organization Society sponsored a summer training course for charity workers in 1898. In 1904 this training course developed into a one-year program of the New York School of Philanthropy, later named the New York School of Social Work.

Work was unmistakably the first-named, namely the new psychology. The ensuing shift in emphasis, from Darwin to Freud, from environmentalism to the psyche, had startling consequences . . .[6]

The Director of the School, Porter R. Lee, who served from 1917 to 1939, was especially interested in the psychological aspects of social work. His main interest was the family and social work's role in relation to it. Yet under his leadership the faculty also taught a wide range of other subjects and faculty members were free to develop different approaches to social work and express their own theories. In 1922 the Russell Sage Foundation gave the School a grant to study social work education. James H. Tufts, professor of philosophy at the University of Chicago, who in 1908 had published *Ethics* jointly with John Dewey, undertook this study and published it in 1923. He pointed out the basic question of social work: should it educate only for adjustment to existing problems, or should it enter the field of prevention and reform? Tufts found that social work was not a single clearly defined field, and he considered it unnecessary at that time to define its scope.

The moral would seem to be that the conception of the field of social work should above all be kept fluid in order to maintain in this profession at least an open mind toward humanity's changing needs and the best methods for meeting them. A profession which seems called upon to supplement in a sense a too narrow professionalism may well be on its guard against itself becoming too professional. And further, a profession which finds one of its distinctive tasks to be that of maintaining an open mind toward humanity's changing needs is not auxiliary in any sense that would imply inferiority in importance.[7]

He recognized the need for the establishment of techniques but he warned against the danger of overloading the curriculum with their study. He saw in the social worker the expert on social problems which "involved ultimate ends and values, and no expertness as to means is a guarantee of just and true perspective for these." [8] The Tufts report had no deep influence on social work education. It

[6] *Ibid.*, pp. 5–7.
[7] James H. Tufts, *Education and Training for Social Work* (New York: Russell Sage Foundation, 1923), p. 31.
[8] *Ibid.*, pp. 166–67.

presented social work and education for social work in the 1920s as a profession still wide and undefined. At this stage experimentation was possible.

Lindeman was added to the faculty mainly because of his thinking about community organization. During this time the School introduced courses in what were then considered "border" areas. For example, George W. Kirchway, head of the department of criminology at Columbia, taught work with delinquents from 1917 to 1929. Not many students specialized in this area but the school administration considered it important to offer a wide variety of experiences and opinions regarding the social work field.

From the beginning Lindeman's courses stressed social work as a part of the social scene and emphasized the relationship between technique and philosophy. In the April 1924 *Bulletin* of the School, his first courses are described as follows:

1924–S.C.W.3. *Social Work and Social Progress*
An evaluation of social work in terms of its relation to the physical, biological and social sciences. A study of social work from the point of view of scientific, ethical and philosophical methods and values. The relation of social work to other factors of progress such as education, government, religion, the labor movement, etc.

1924–S.C.W.4. *Social Psychology*
A study of individual behavior which is a response to the social environment together with an approach to the study of the behavior of groups. Emphasis is placed upon analysis of instances of unadjustment with an attempt to clarify the social worker's function as a factor in social control.

1926–S.C.W.3. *Social Technique and Social Ethics*
A course designed to acquaint the student with methods for evaluating social techniques and programs in the light of ethics. Actual cases involving problems of ethical decision will be utilized as the basis for discussion. The aim of the course is primarily to assist students in the process of evolving a social philosophy.

Lindeman was an inspired teacher. In talking with his former students one is struck by the enthusiasm with which they speak of him. A constantly recurring remark was that he was the most stimulating teacher they had had in school. Obviously students were not only engrossed with the content of his courses but also stimulated by the way in which he taught. They always felt that he made them *think*: they never had to accept dogmatic statements; on the contrary they were forced to do their own thinking and to challenge their teacher's theories.

It is characteristic that in his philosophy class Lindeman emphasized his belief in the importance of eugenics and birth control. This, of course, is contrary to the teaching of the Catholic Church. Yet some of his students were priests who later rose to important positions in the Catholic Church — Father Thomas Brennack, for instance, and Monsignor Robert Keegan, who became the executive of Catholic Charities of the Archdiocese of New York. They did not agree and they challenged Lindeman's position, but they maintained a good relationship with him. Many students felt that Lindeman never *talked* democracy but that he *practiced* democracy. In no other class did they feel so completely free to express themselves.

He was able to draw out the shy student. One of his former students said, "We were actually freed in his classes." [9] Lester Granger, today the Executive Director of the National Urban League and one of Lindeman's early students, said that Lindeman's greatest achievement was his capacity to *teach*. To Lindeman, teaching was a mutual learning process between teacher and student, between supervisor and worker. Granger remembered that there was never a remoteness in Lindeman, but that every student felt like an equal and was inspired to do his best. He considered Lindeman one of the best discussion leaders in class or in community groups.[10]

Lindeman himself felt that students were collaborators, not people beneath him. It was typical of him to write, "It happens that I'm now collaborating with several of my students on a theme . . ." [11] One of his colleagues, Margaret Leal, called him an "enabling peda-

[9] Interview with Halina Korsak.

[10] Granger remembered a discussion Lindeman led in 1928 in Camden, New Jersey. The participants were people of high standing in the community and they were "stiff" in their relationships. Lindeman suggested that they get up, move in a circle, touch each other, and speak to each other. When some protested that it made them feel foolish, Lindeman laughingly said, "It is good for anybody to feel foolish for a change, it makes us less solemn." This was his way of shaking people out of their complacency.

[11] Lindeman, *Leisure — A National Issue. Planning for the Leisure of a Democratic People* (New York: Association Press, 1939), p. 10.

gogue." She said that he could always work with imaginative students, but that those who had no imagination and were used to dogmatic thinking gained little from him. He influenced those students who liked the exercise of philosophy and those who realized that his contribution was to make them think harder. Miss Leal said that he was "a shock and a help," especially to the foreign student, since his approach was different from that of other teachers in that he forced them to express their own ideas. He helped people to talk clearly and to listen to others. He asked questions and tried to get discussion beyond the obvious — beyond the idea that everything is black and white. He had a conscious desire to carry students to the point where they learned to recognize true controversies and to distinguish them from fabricated ones.[12] Charlotte K. Demorest summarized this: "Eduard's method of teaching was a direct result of his belief in the mountain-potential in his fellow-adults. He quite simply persuaded you to teach yourself, to learn along with him." [13]

Lindeman was one of a remarkable collection of teachers — a collection perhaps best seen through his lively descriptions of them in his "Interpretative History of the New York School of Social Work." And the descriptions will show at the same time his genuine enjoyment of diverse personalities and diverse ideas.

Porter Lee was a complicated personality. His chronic illness compelled him to be absent at frequent intervals. He was always half-administrator and half-teacher, and I surmise that it was the latter half which really predominated although he finally and reluctantly abandoned teaching altogether. As administrator he "made room" for the expanding pressures of specialization but his personal philosophy remained "generic"; he was, in other words, more deeply attached to the common elements in social work than to its specialized and fractional compartmentalizations. His teaching method was informal and experimental. For example, in his principal course on the Family he used fiction as collateral reading and contemporary novels were discussed in class as sources of insight respecting family life. His was a warm, genial personality surrounded by a curious reserve. Although we were at this stage an intimate

[12] Interview with Margaret Leal, March 2, 1955.

[13] Charlotte K. Demorest, "He Saw the Mountain in the Molehill," *20th Anniversary Yearbook of Adult Education*, New York Adult Education Council, 1953, p. 18.

group, it cannot be truthfully said that any of us really felt that we knew more than a fraction of the whole which was Porter Lee.

Walter Pettit, also a combined administrator-teacher, was the "outgoingest" personality in this group. I still recall bursts of hilarious laughter which emanated from his class-room resounding down the hallways. He was completely informal in manner. Students attached themselves to him as counselor and friend. As already indicated, he introduced a new teaching method in his courses on Community Organization. Instead of leading students to an understanding of community processes by discussing these processes in the abstract, he required his students to begin by studying actual events in real communities. In other words, he introduced the "case study" method into the field of community organization, and after some years of experimentation along these lines, published a book of community case records.

George Kirchway, the oldest member of this teaching staff, had brought to the School a rich body of experiences previously gained at Sing Sing prison. He was what is now commonly called an "old-fashioned American liberal," which means that he was firmly attached to certain principles of justice and rightness. Always impeccably dressed and always prepared to enter upon a debate, he gave the appearance of a scholarly gentleman visiting in a home in which he was never completely certain of his welcome. His speech was precise and carried a certain quality of literary reference. His lectures were delightfully informative, interspersed with humor and dramatic anecdote. Other teachers were at this time experimenting with newer teaching methods in which increased student participation through discussion was sought but Kirchway went his own way, taught as an authority, as indeed he was, and thus proudly faded from the scene. After his retirement the courses he taught were dropped from the curriculum.

Kate Claghorn had the distinction of having been one of the students in the original class which met for instruction in the summer of 1898 under the direction of Philip Ayres. As was true of so many persons in social work at this stage, she was motivated by the dual incentive of humanitarian impulses on the one hand and a scientific compulsion on the other. Fortunately, the School furnished channels for both incentives: she gave courses in Statistics and Problems of the Immigrant. She had a passion for exactness and at a time when the social sciences were manifesting a tendency to emulate the methods of the older and more exact physical sciences she represented in this group the growing demand for quantitative reliability.

Marion Kenworthy had the effect upon the School of a medium-sized gale disturbing the academic waters. Her introductory course in Psychiatry sent students into eddies of disturbance which necessitated basic reorientations of their backgrounds and experiences. Changing the metaphor abruptly, Marion Kenworthy at this stage acted as a detonator setting off explosions which had a profound effect upon the School and upon social work in general. Freud, it must be remembered, had not yet been popularized. A few writers here and there were beginning to incorporate Freudian concepts in fiction and in criticism but on the whole it seems safe to say that psychoanalytical ideas had not yet been incorporated in our culture. Marion Kenworthy was, and is, a gifted teacher who, like most of her contemporaries in social work education, knew how to transmute actual case material into living reality and insight. She also taught as one having authority.

Sarah Ivins was at this time still teaching case work but was already on the threshold of her new career as director of Field Work for the School. It was in this latter capacity that she made a fundamental contribution to social work education. The New York School of Social Work developed under her guidance a system of Field Work which still stands as a model. It was her contention that the work performed by students while attached to the social agencies of the community was of equal importance with class-room studies. She insisted that students who could not adapt themselves to the rigorous conditions of actual performance should not be permitted to become practicing social workers. Meticulous, thorough-going application was her watchword.

Philip Klein, while at this period devoting his major energies to research, was already beginning to give indication of skills in expository teaching. Like most of his colleagues, he was liberal in temperament and motivated by solid convictions. Always ready for argument, indeed usually the instigator of debate, his presence meant that faculty meetings never lacked excitement. There was an impish quality in his makeup which I am happy to state has persisted and which leads to unpredictable consequences. With respect to pedagogical content, he has persistently and consistently struggled to supplement the practical features of the curriculum with a deeper understanding of the nature of the society in which social agencies operate.

John Fitch, one of the first labor economists of his generation, owed his primary allegiance to facts. Intellectual integrity was the cornerstone of his character. The emerging professional nomenclature, sometimes referred to as jargon, emanating from case work and psychiatry puzzled and perplexed him. His attitude towards education was derived from his conception of what a true university should be, namely, a place where students learn to respect tested knowledge. His devotion to strict standards permeated his teaching, his writing and his role as responsible member of a teaching group.

Gordon Hamilton, already showing that promise of brilliance which was to characterize her career as one of the most creative teachers of modern case work, taught as one having a mission. A rare combination of theory and practice led her to both inclusiveness and inventiveness. New ideas were being constantly incorporated in her outlook and her method. She had a lively interest in pedagogy as a growing science as well as a practical art. The newer insights of psychiatry became important ingredients in the content of her courses. Her mind had, and has, a subtle quality which is difficult to define except as a factor of unpredictability.

Henry Thurston was an affectionate, humane and cultured person whose love of people was matched by love of nature. When he brought flowers from his New Jersey garden as presents to his colleagues there was a warm light in his eyes, the delight of him who gives of himself. Sincerity of purpose and devotion to high aims made him a source of inspiration to his students and his fellow teachers. Among his high aims was his attachment to the notion that the chief objective of institutions caring for children was useful citizenship. Even after his retirement he set to work on a final book which was to serve as guide to teachers of the young and to child welfare workers.

A few of the teachers belonging to this group will be here omitted and for two reasons, namely: space and the fact that I knew them less intimately and have with respect to them less of a sense of reliable recollection. But I must add the name of Antoinette Cannon who was most certainly one of the major influences of this epoch. Her special interest was Medical Social Work, a field in which she was a pioneer. Her sphinx-like calm was deceptive. Her feelings ran deeply. And she was possessed of great wisdom, the kind of wisdom which comes in part from the heart. Fear was alien to her way of life and as she grew older her liberal and generous temperament seemed to expand and deepen.

At the time this group of full-time teachers was at work laying the foundations for the School's second quarter-century span another group of part-time teachers and lecturers of special note labored by their side. It should be noted for example, that during the year 1928–1929 special lectures were given by Harry Hopkins, Solomon Lowenstein, Thomas L. Brennack, Amy Hewes, Mary Arnold and Edith S. King. Also, during this same year, courses were offered by Otto Rank, Leonard Mayo, Shelby Harrison, Robert Lansdale, Grace Marcus, Arthur Dunham, Elwood Street, the Routzahns (Evart and Mary) and a score of others who later became prominent in social work. Altogether, this was probably one of the most remarkable collections of seasoned and young social workers involved in professional training to be found anywhere on the continent.[14]

Lindeman's interests and teachings were not confined to the School of Social Work. His outside activities included leading discussions, lecturing all over the country, and writing. He enjoyed working with professionals as well as with lay people. In 1926–1927, he was a director of research for the Workers Education Bureau of America; 1927–1940, chairman of the Hunterton Library Commission, New Jersey; 1929–1933, consultant to the National Council of Parent Education; he was used in labor mediation by Standard Oil, New Jersey. He was active in the adult education movement.

His book, *Social Education*, published in 1933, was an account of the endeavor of the Inquiry to investigate basic questions of human relations.[15] The same year, with John Hader, he published *Dynamic Social Research*, also born out of the endeavor of the Inquiry. The book was mainly concerned with group process and social research.[16] The research was done on joint committees of employers and employees in company unions. Hader and Lindeman were interested in developing a methodology of research into group relations and in learning how to work with committees which presented group conflicts.[17]

Lindeman's lectures took him all over the country. He was a dynamic speaker. A listener commented about his speeches, "They were like sparks and one felt his sincerity." Some of his colleagues criticized him for doing too much speaking, while others felt that the contribution he made in those speeches helped greatly to interpret social work's goals and to increase the prestige of the School.

[14] Lindeman, "The New York School of Social Work, An Interpretative History," Chapter V (unpublished), pp. 16–25.

[15] Lindeman, *Social Education* (New York: New Republic, Inc., 1933).

[16] John J. Hader and Eduard C. Lindeman, *Dynamic Social Research* (New York: Harcourt, 1933).

[17] For a detailed discussion, see pp. 131–32.

Lindeman himself felt two ways about this activity. He apparently enjoyed the recognition he gained; it probably made up for much of the deprivation in youth and helped to satisfy his secret yearning for friendship. He had difficulty in establishing close individual relationships. In the large group he could give more freely of himself. Yet he was also afraid of crowds. He did not let many people know this but he confided it to his close friend, Thomas Cotton. Cotton accompanied him on many of his engagements and often saved him from the crowds by helping him get out of a meeting when people searched him out for too long a time. With the sensitivity of a faithful friend Cotton recognized when Lindeman became overtired. Yet sometimes Thomas Cotton's task was a thankless one because Eduard Lindeman was incapable of sparing himself or of saying "no" to requests. Cotton was sometimes sharply rebuked when he tried to slow Lindeman down.[18]

In 1925 Lindeman underwent a thyroid operation at Johns Hopkins. While recuperating, he took his family abroad to Italy, France, and England. Little writing was done during the trip, since he was still weak from the operation, and all four girls came down with measles while the family was in Italy, but in general the family felt stimulated by the trip.

His intense curiosity about people and the social scene led to more trips. In 1929 he was in France, Italy, Germany, and England. He had entered his daughter Betty in Dartington Hall, an experimental school founded by Mr. and Mrs. Leonard K. Elmhirst (Mrs. Elmhirst was the former Dorothy Whitney Straight). He visited Betty and studied the modern educational methods used in Dartington Hall. In 1932 he went to Russia to observe their experimental communism.

[18] Interview with Thomas Cotton, April 13, 1955. Thomas Cotton is Chairman of the Adult Education Council of New York City.

CHAPTER 3

SOCIAL ACTION AND CURRICULUM PLANNING

With the depression and the emergent reforms of the Roosevelt administration, Lindeman became increasingly involved in government services. In 1934 he became the consulting director of the Division of Recreation of the Works Progress Administration. He described this experience and his resulting thinking in a book published in 1939, *Leisure — A National Issue. Planning for the Leisure of a Democratic People.* He considered leisure-time planning a part of social policy. He never looked upon recreation as an empty passing of time; rather, he believed that leisure provided an opportunity for people to feel free; he felt that they should learn to exercise their democratic responsibilities during the hours they were not forced to work for a living. He recognized the need for people to work but he also believed that during the period of unemployment it was the responsibility of the government to help them to become capable of using their free time. But he never considered this a substitute for gainful employment. He saw the individual and cultural implications of constructive use of leisure time. His friendship with Harry Hopkins meant that he had easy access to the White House (he was invited to the White House several times). Hopkins recognized the social importance of the WPA recreation project. It is typical of Lindeman's application of theory to practice that he said in the introduction to his book: "In the past four years I have enjoyed an opportunity which does not come to a teacher often, especially a teacher of philosophy: I have worked as a civil servant with an agency so new, so unique and so daring as to preclude all reliance upon precedent, namely the Works Progress Administration."

During these years Lindeman became interested in the problem of *planning* for social services and in the relationship between freedom and planning. In July 1932, the faculty of the School of Social Work — troubled by the implications of the depression — called a one-day conference of which Lindeman was the chairman. The summary of this institute is significant in that it shows Lindeman's practical application of philosophy and the influence it had on the faculty's thinking.

The subject, "Perspectives in Social Work," was an attempt to put everyday problems into a larger framework. He explained perspective as "the art of setting partial or fractional ideas against the wholes to which they belong, of moving from specific ideas through generalizations, through deduction, of placing an activity in a rational content, of viewing the traits of an individual in the light of the group to which he belongs." In his introduction he discussed the necessity of establishing new goals in social work because of the new social situation. The faculty raised, among other problems, the question of whether social work was "merely an ambulatory service" or whether it should come to "rejection of all palliatives in favor of reform or possible revolution." In the midst of violent disagreement on these questions, Lindeman was able to bring the discussion back to the consideration of possible alternatives and to integration of different methods.

The pressures now being exerted upon them because of the critical economic situation in which the nation finds itself imply a still greater preoccupation with the details of the daily task. But, it is precisely now, that perspectives are needed; in the midst of this crisis we should be finding the incentives for viewing our tasks in more comprehensive terms . . . and if we are to go henceforth in a new direction as a people we shall need to draw heavily upon the foresight and upon the insight of those who are capable of thinking clearly when confusion reigns.

He made several proposals: there should be no more laissez faire; groups should assume more leadership.

Dictatorship either of an individual or of a small group is inevitable unless we learn how to develop the arts of collective control, leadership, and administration. . . . It is not enough to possess a social goal. We need also social methods, since a true social end may only be achieved through the instrumentality of valid social means. . . . The instrument of social administration is conference. Those who will be prepared for the new era of social planning and social control will be those who have acquired the art of conferencing; those who have learned how to substitute for aggressiveness and power the satisfactions of shared experience, and shared responsibility.[1]

These ideas had grown out of his contact with Mary Parker Follett and his participation in an informal group of educators and social workers who were studying the methods of democratic leadership in small groups and who worked on the understanding of group relations. The interest had come from the youth-serving agencies, the community centers, adult education, and, later, the settlement houses.

The "group work method" was slowly developed during this time in close relationship to community organization, progressive education, and a strong interest in reform and social action. It began to be taught in a few schools of social work. Outstanding among their leaders were Wilber Newstetter who had come to Western Reserve in 1932 from religious education, and Clara Kaiser and Grace Coyle, who came from social work with strong backgrounds in labor relations and the industrial department of the YWCA. In 1935 Clara Kaiser went to the New York School of Social Work specifically to teach group work, thus starting a fruitful cooperation with Lindeman.

In those years before the Second World War Lindeman's active participation in national and state organizations was enormous. His work with the WPA projects increased. He was chairman of the National Share Croppers Fund in New York, consultant to the National Council of Parent Education, president of the New Jersey State Conference of Social Work, chairman of the New Jersey Library Planning Commission and the New Jersey Social Planning Commission, board member of the Council against Intolerance, adviser to the magazine *Rural America*, member of the Advisory Committee to the White House Conference on Children in a Democracy, member of the Committee on Research and Education of the Federal Council of Churches of New York City, director of the

---

[1] Lindeman, "Perspectives in Social Work," *Bulletin of the New York School of Social Work*, July 1932, pp. 5, 8, 12, 13.

Service for Intercultural Education, director of the Association on American Indian Affairs. In 1940 he became trustee of a settlement house — the Hudson Guild in New York, of the National Urban League, and of Briar Cliff Junior College and Adelphi College.

Lindeman's outside activities took him away from the School of Social Work a great deal — perhaps too much — during this period. Several of his colleagues commented on his lack of interest in social work concerns, especially those related to methods; yet he took part in some important new developments. He was one of the early group of practitioners and teachers who developed the intensive use of group work and established parts of its theory. He continued his interest in community organization, though his teaching was more and more concerned with philosophy.

Lindeman never was close to the development of the casework method. His fear of intimacy must have played a part in this. But when it came to the thinking through of the philosophical basis for casework, he was interested. Lucille Austin's "The Evolution of Our Casework Concepts" was certainly influenced in its philosophy by Lindeman, with whom she discussed these problems. Two warring schools of thought had developed in casework: the functional school — based on the theories of Rank, the psychiatrist, and the diagnostic school — based on Freudian theory. In her article, Mrs. Austin related Rank's thinking to the idealistic schools of Hegel and Kant. According to her, their emphasis was on constant change and on fear as a basic motivation for action. Freud's theory was more closely related to the German empiricists' and American pragmatists'. His determinism, which was attacked by the functional school, she explained as a flexible concept of cause and effect, having "no more absolute significance in psychology and the social sciences than it has in the physical sciences. Scientific laws mean greater probability — probability great enough to serve as a guide for action. . . . just as the law of heredity allows for mutation, so psychological determinism provides for variations." [2]

[2] Lucille Nickel Austin, "The Evolution of Our Casework Concepts," *The Family*, Vol. XX, No. 2, April 1939. Mrs. Austin discussed Lindeman's influence on this article in an interview with the author, January 17, 1955.

The outgrowth of such flexible determinism was the conviction of the diagnostic school that the worker could know something about the client's problems, past and present. People were individually different (this coincided with the functional school's beliefs) but there were similarities among them which could serve as hypotheses for diagnosis. As an argument against the functionalists who placed greatest emphasis on the client's self-determination, Mrs. Austin concluded that the social worker could and had to take responsibility — though he had to guard himself against feelings of omnipotence. As authority for this philosophy, she cited Dewey, who accepted the individuality and creativeness of the students, but believed that the teacher should also influence the student.

Mrs. Austin's article was a refutation of the nondirective method and of individualization so great that it did not allow for scientific investigation. A discussion of whether or not she did justice to the functional point of view is not pertinent to this study, but it should be pointed out that her relating Freud to American pragmatism is highly questionable. What is important here is that she tried to find a philosophical base for differences among the psychological views of the human being and for casework methods, and that Lindeman influenced her thinking on these subjects.

In 1937 Walter Pettit, a close friend of Lindeman who shared his interest in community organization and in public services, became director of the New York School. In a special effort to interest and involve Lindeman more in the affairs of the school, he appointed him chairman of a curriculum study which started in 1937 and was carried through under the succeeding chairmanships of Lindeman, Grace White, and Clara Kaiser. The basic questions from the beginning were (1) What weight should be given to courses which are technical as distinguished from those which are either orientational or quasi-technical? (2) In what order should technical courses be arranged?[3] These of course involved the question of the relative weights of methods courses and information courses.

The Committee on Social Forces of the Curriculum Study was

[3] Lindeman, "New York School of Social Work," Chapter VII (unpublished), p. 5.

chaired by Porter Lee; Lindeman was one of the ten members. The preliminary report stated: "Social work entered the period of the depression with an organizational development firmly grounded in the past traditions of social welfare and at the peak of its efficiency. It had reached also the period of its most highly developed technical competence." [4]

The problem which presented itself in 1936 and in the following years was a result of the fact that social work had become a highly diversified field: the question arose as to how to teach all these different aspects. By 1939, therefore, it was considered necessary to evolve a plan for the progressive development of the curriculum. Eduard Lindeman was the chairman of the continued study at this time. The first document he presented to the curriculum committee showed his typical approach to problems: he raised alternatives, stated his preference, and then left the decision to the committee. He began by asking the committee to decide upon the method of approach to be used. He saw four alternatives: an analysis of criticism of the existing curriculum, an appraisal of work performed by previous curriculum committees, a study of the actual tasks performed by social workers to see how the demands of the practice correlated with the content of the existing curriculum, or to "begin by positing the theory of professional education including the outline of an ideal curriculum, and then proceed to formulate a plan which will approximate this ideal."

Lindeman preferred the last approach. In establishing a theory of education he presented two alternatives: either looking upon professional education as a unit in and of itself and disconnected from all other varieties of education, or "assuming that the education of an individual is a totality, or at least, a unifying experience in which professional education is merely a part, although an integral part." He tended toward the theory of education as a unified experience and outlined a sequence like the following: *Elementary and secondary education* consists of physical education, the arts, the humanities, and such intellectual studies as mathematics and the sciences. *Higher*

[4] "A Preliminary Report on Curriculum Study," May 18, 1936 (mimeographed), p. 3.

education is a further elaboration of the same general content, with the introduction of new courses designed to be either vocational or pre-vocational. *Professional education* is a process of relating previous learning to a specific profession and its requirements — plus training in specific techniques.[5]

He enlarged on this sequence by pointing out that all the teachers would have to be aware continuously of what had gone before in other parts of the curriculum and what was to come. Teachers in a professional school should demonstrate knowledge of the practice of their profession. They should also be able to relate it to the arts, humanities, and sciences previously explored. The professional school should make a constant effort to relate social theory to social practice and current economic situations should be discussed in the light of economic theory.

Consequently, following his theory of organic process in everything undertaken, he suggested closer integration between class and field work. He proposed that new thinking about curriculum should arise out of practice, out of research, and out of new hypotheses suggested by teachers of theory. These were interacting processes and therefore curriculum-building should consider all three sources.

There are many who now claim that there is but one sound method for building professional curricula, namely by first studying the field of practice, by making job analyses of the practitioners and then proceeding to construct a course of study which will equip students to perform the operations demanded by the field. There are others who insist that such a procedure would soon reduce all professional training schools to the status of adjuncts to field work supervision, and that the intellectual content of this type of training would be bound to be retrogressive.[6]

The deliberations of the curriculum committee became very practical on the subject of a proposed course which would add to the students' knowledge of the social environment. Some of the faculty felt that the curriculum was overweighted with technique courses and that students did not learn enough about social issues and the

---

[5] Memo from Lindeman to the curriculum committee, June 14, 1939 (typewritten), pp. 1, 2.

[6] *Ibid.*, p. 3.

social scene out of which these issues arose. In 1949, proposals for
"Course X" were worked out by three members of the faculty: John
Fitch, who was closely identified with the labor movement, Philip
Klein, who had successfully directed the famous Pittsburgh Survey,
and Eduard Lindeman, who tried to synthesize Fitch's and Klein's
proposals. The memorandum setting forth the proposals was significant because it showed different approaches to the problem of a
background course for social workers. It was divided into three
parts: (1) purposes which Course X was presumed to meet, (2) material to be included as content for Course X, and (3) proposed methods for presenting Course X. Under each heading each of the three
faculty members listed his proposals. They all seemed to agree on
the purpose of the course. All three asked for an increased orientation toward the social environment. Klein's proposal went farthest
into preparation for actual use of the information. He suggested
training of social workers as participants in social action movements.

Their respective suggestions for material to be included in Course
X most clearly bring out the differences among the three men; these
suggestions are included here for that reason and for their historical
interest.

According to Fitch, material on the following subjects ought to be
included: (1) social, economic, and political problems; (2) principles, agencies, and practices — public and private — for dealing
with these problems; and (3) programs and philosophies. Under
social problems the course would include material on (a) elements
in the social structure: racial, religious, economic, and regional
groupings, (b) the adjustment of these groups to each other and
barriers to an integrated society, (c) discriminatory practices with
respect to aliens, immigrants, Negroes, Jews, Catholics, Jehovah's
Witnesses, etc., (d) the effect of exclusive organizations based on
ancestry, nationality, religion, etc., (e) causes and effects of illiteracy and semiliteracy; and (f) the nature and meaning of tolerance.

Economic problems would consist of (a) maldistribution of
wealth and income, (b) low wages and work interruptions, (c) effect
of low income on housing and diet, (d) growth of the corporation
and disappearance of the individual entrepreneur, (e) relation of the

corporation to individual enterprise and to employment relations, and (f) the business cycle.

Under the heading *political problems* would be considered (a) the basic structure of American government, division of powers, nature of legislatures and courts, states' rights, (b) constitutional obstacles to the enactment of social legislation, (c) limitations on the right to vote or to support political heresies, as for example, poll tax, outlawing of Communist party, etc., and (d) political and economic illiteracy.

The *principles, agencies, and practices* for dealing with these problems would include (a) the Federal Constitution, with emphasis on the Bill of Rights, (b) the administrative departments of the Federal government and their services, (c) similar state and municipal services with emphasis on education and training of the handicapped, vocational education and guidance, legal aid services, housing, etc., (d) legislative enactments to effect economic change, such as minimum wage, placement, social insurance, (e) self-help agencies such as cooperatives, trade unions, tenant organizations, agencies for workers or adult education, and (f) agencies for the promotion of social legislation and improved administration.

Programs and philosophies would be within the existing sociopolitical structure and would extend existing services and promote new programs such as greater activity of government in economic life, and social and economic planning. They would be designed to effect fundamental changes in the social structure itself — all proposed "roads to freedom."

According to Klein, material which ought to be included as content for Course X could be organized under the following headings: (1) conditions of livelihood, (2) supplementary measures and resources for livelihood, (3) the national economy, and (4) related problems.

Conditions of livelihood would cover the source, nature, and security of income from wages and farm salary; the relation of this income to standards of living, to vocational problems of children and youth, and to the composition and internal life of the changing family.

Supplementary measures and resources for livelihood should cover conditions and extent of suspended income due to illness, unemployment, old age, excess fertility, stranded occupations and areas, etc., and should cover the measures of supplementation such as the entire fields of public assistance and social insurance. Both this subject matter and that under conditions of livelihood should be regarded from the standpoint of the citizen or potential client as well as that of the actual beneficiary or client; it should, in other words, *be a socioeconomic analysis, not a client classification.*

The national economy determines the conditions of livelihood and the supplementary measures and resources for livelihood. Here the course should cover the major industrial-occupational characteristics of the country and its subdivisions; changing relations between production and consumption; something about the meaning of domestic and foreign markets; some of the basic relations between taxation, banking, investment, and prosperity; and some of the major theories for reconstruction of the national economy.

Related to these, but dealt with through the program-making or "institutional" perspective, there should be included the more practical and realistic aspects of (a) politics and political-governmental programs, (b) the labor movement in its larger relations, and (c) governmental programs of public welfare and the relations of policy and administration of these to the general philosophies of voluntary enterprise, community life, and social work organization.

The foci for dealing with the subject matter suggested should be two: facts and issues. Facts should be regarded principally as they represent the changing situation, and issues should be discussed as cross-sections between fact and philosophy. This mode of focusing the discussion could be applied to every part of the subject matter, and should be made concrete by relating it to sponsoring bodies of social action programs and governmental services.

Lindeman proposed that the content of Course X be divided into (1) historical perspectives, (2) an inventory of the contemporary situation, (3) plans and programs for future progress, and (4) the role of the United States in world affairs.

The *historical perspectives* would involve (a) the American people and their habitat from several viewpoints: from the point of view of ethnology — who are they? where did they come from? are they becoming a type? what are their characteristics? what is their birth rate? how is their health?; from the viewpoint of ecology — where do they live? why do they live there? what is the nature of regional differences? what are the natural resources there? what are the human resources there? is there cultural pluralism?; and from the point of view of ways of life and living — what is the urban pattern of life? what is the rural pattern of life? what is the suburban pattern of life? what is social mobility like? what and where are the "blighted" areas?

Also involved in historical perspectives would be (b) the structure of American society which would include political federalism — the units of government and the relation between those units; economic forms — individual entrepreneurs, companies and corporations, private and public banks, business associations, trade unions; and social organization — as affected by racial differences, as determined by religious differences, and as derived from class differences.

Another facet of historical perspectives would be (c) the evolution of American democracy: the historic symbols of American democracy, sources of democratic ideas, the persistently anti-democratic forces, and crises in the democratic struggle.

The *inventory of the contemporary situation* would list (a) economic assets and liabilities of productive capacity, the national debt, the tax burden, the distribution of wealth and income, and the dynamics of technology; (b) basic maladjustments in American life — unemployment, problems of children, youth, and the aged, barriers to learning and culture, physical and mental disease, and crime and delinquency; and (c) chronic conflicts — racial, religious, regional, industrial, and professional — in American life.

Plans and programs for future progress would include discussions of the future of the federal government and the economic process — agriculture, industry, banking and investments, credit, unemployment, labor, the handicapped; of private agencies and institutions — church programs for social action, casework social agencies, group work social agencies, agencies promoting fact-finding and fact-dissemination, and agencies promoting social, economic, and educational legislation. This part of the proposed course would discuss steps toward social, economic, and cultural planning that could be taken within the democratic process; it would also discuss other ideological programs of reform — socialism, Communism, and Fascism.[7]

Klein's proposal was most closely related to practice. Lindeman added historical perspective and philosophical thought but did not integrate enough methodological thinking.

In the further deliberations of the curriculum committee it became clear that the faculty was searching for a way to bring technical and nontechnical courses closer together. They hoped that each individual teacher would try to combine the two in his own teaching — as the following, from the committee's Interim Report, suggests: "Mr. Lindeman to teach a course in the general field of education dealing primarily with educational methods as related to group work (group work sequence)." The Interim Report further shows Lindeman's constant attempt to apply his principle of education as an organic unit and his principle of differentiation in unity. "So far as possible a curriculum should move in the direction of organic unity, its parts should bear a necessary relation to the whole. The whole should represent an inner congruity." [8]

The members of the committee recognized the difficulty of achieving this in social work, where there were many specializations and highly diversified agencies. The committee expressed the hope that Course X would help to integrate some of these diversities and furnish background to technical courses. But while they asked for unity they sounded a warning against conformity.

A danger which inheres in a too-highly integrated curriculum is the tendency of its faculty to become an indoctrinating bloc. Social theory which is not in advance of social practice becomes a justification of established practice whereas one of its major functions should be to challenge practice, to open channels of invention. A faculty without dissenters is likely to wither and die from within. On the

[7] Memorandum concerning proposed Course X, April 11, 1941, pp. 2–7.

[8] "Interim Report of the Curriculum Committee for Faculty Council Meeting," June 9, 1941, pp. 1, 2.

other hand, a faculty which is preoccupied with dissension is likely to find itself outstripped by other schools traveling in the direction of unity. The principle here involved seems to be that health resides in the consciousness of movement towards integration accompanied by the assumption that complete unity is not desirable.[9]

The curriculum that was finally contrived after many years was based on five principles:

1. It is not the aim of the School to train highly specialized practitioners but rather persons capable of functioning in the broad and general field of Social Work.

2. It is the aim of the School to prepare social workers for service in both public and voluntary social agencies.

3. There exists a central core of knowledge which should form the common background of all students and this core includes both technical and non-technical material.

4. Certain content is essential for special areas of practice particularly in the three fields of casework, group work and community organization.

5. The curriculum should also provide for electives which will meet the needs of experienced students, and which will allow for greater flexibility in planning the courses of study of younger students.[10]

[9] *Ibid.*, p. 3.
[10] Lindeman, "New York School of Social Work," Chapter VII (unpublished), pp. 7–8.

CHAPTER 4

THE PROBLEMS OF WORLD WAR II AND ITS AFTERMATH

THE outbreak of the Second World War brought new problems, new concerns, and involvement in new and different activities. One of his problems was reconciling his humanitarian views with the cruel necessities of war. When, early in the war, former President Hoover was seeking support for his opposition to Roosevelt's and Churchill's plan to withhold food from enemy countries, Lindeman wrote to Mrs. Marion Beers Howden:

The worst pressure I have had to bear in recent months has come from the Hoover Committee. They insist on having my name for their committee and I cannot bring myself to sign. But, it is so difficult: I don't want people to starve, Germans, not any people. And yet food must be regarded now as a weapon. How many things we do these days in contradiction to both logic and our better selves! [1]

He also had to come to terms with the question of pacifism. Although his closest friend, Roger Baldwin, was a pacifist, Lindeman recognized the great danger of Nazism and the importance of resisting it. Accordingly, he made his decision.

Prof. Eduard C. Lindeman, of the New York School of Social Work, and Prof. Paul H. Douglas, of the University of Chicago, said today they had resigned from the board of directors of the Institute for Propaganda Analysis because it was too critical of President Roosevelt's defense policies. Lindeman said he expected to take active part in the defense program soon. He said he was "all out for

[1] Letter in possession of Robert Gessner.

the intervention" and that the institute "doesn't seem to be." Douglas said the institute's bulletins were too critical of the Administration to suit him. . . .[2]

He recognized the danger of loss of civil liberties during wartime and sounded an early warning in a speech to the Detroit New Century Club of which the *Detroit Free Press* said:

Calling himself "a discouraged optimist," the head of the social philosophy department at the New York School of Social Work, explained that he had come "a long, tortuous path of logic and conscience to arrive at the conclusion that we should help England" and had finally decided that the world would be a better place after the war if England wins.

He warned against the danger of loss of civil liberties in this country but said that he was not worried about our losing our social reforms.

"In times like these," he said, "we nibble away at the Bill of Rights. We may try to keep a Communist or Bundist from saying his say and in doing so we are apt to put off our own avenues of expression."

Most important consideration for Americans in his opinion is to figure out what kind of a society we want after the war. Among points to be considered he listed better housing, medical attention and better food for everyone.[3]

During the war years Lindeman commuted to New York, often staying with Roger Baldwin. By 1942, the house in New Jersey seemed to have grown too large, because three of the daughters had married. Ruth, the second daughter, had married first, in 1937; she was the only one who stayed in New Jersey. In May 1938, Doris had married Robert Gessner, a writer and teacher, and two months later Betty married a young lawyer with whom she moved to Minnesota. The only one left at home was the youngest, Barbara, who was married a few years later in New York.

In the early forties the Lindemans moved into a modern apartment house in New York only a few blocks from the School, which was at that time situated on East 22nd Street.

Lindeman established closer relationships with his colleagues at

[2] *Detroit News* (Detroit, Mich., May 31, 1941).
[3] *Detroit Free Press* (Detroit, Mich., February 4, 1941).

the School, and his interest and concern with specific issues of social work increased. He made a conscious effort to integrate his philosophical thinking with social work methods, especially group work and community organization. This is reflected in his 1943 proposal to change one of his courses. He had formerly taught a course called Conflict and Integration. He now suggested offering a new course on the principles involved in group work, community organization, and social planning. He gave as reasons for changing course content his feelings that (1) the former course was too theoretical and not sufficiently focused upon contemporary situations; (2) students were not primarily concerned with systems of philosophy but rather interested in philosophy as an aid to solving everyday problems; (3) all courses should be more definitely related to the technical core of the School's curriculum. The new course should offer an opportunity for bringing philosophic considerations into closer relations with technical problems.

The following outline of this course indicates the way in which philosophical thinking penetrated his teaching:

1. Group work as a field of social work; its interrelations with casework and community organization.

2. Varieties of groups considered from the viewpoint of functions.

3. Ways of observing or studying group behavior: behavioristic; cultural; psycho-social; technical (procedures) — as means; functional — as ends; philosophic — as means plus ends; psychiatric — as challenge to individual autonomy.

4. Group work as an element in the democratic process: judge versus jury, parliament versus king, association versus leader.

5. Philosophic problems involved in the act of leadership.

6. Groups in communities — a community as a congeries of groups.

7. Autonomous versus managed groups.

8. Anthropological approach to the study of primitive and sophisticated communities.

9. The development of the modern sense of community.

10. Forces tending to disrupt contemporary communities.

11. Theories of community organization.

12. The community as a microcosmic society.
13. The rise of the planning concept.
14. Planning as an instrument of dictatorship.
15. Planning within a democratic setting.
16. The content of social planning.
17. Planning as an exercise in values.
18. The group as an instrument of planning.
19. Ecological considerations precipitated by planning.
20. The integration of science and philosophy in social planning.

When the New York School was asked, early in the war, to assume some of the responsibility for preparing graduate students in social work for work in foreign countries after the war, Lindeman's interest was widened to include the international community. He was delegated to visit the School of International Administration at Columbia University to find out what the New York School's part in the undertaking should be. As a result of this visit, he suggested that the New York School teach two units of work, each twelve weeks long. "One of these units will deal with problems of the individual and will include psychiatry, health, casework, etc. The other unit will deal with administrative problems connected with this type of administration and will be primarily community organization and group work material."[4]

Both these documents — the one dealing with the course in philosophy of group work, community organization, and social planning, and the other with international problems — were indications of Lindeman's increased identification with social work and the concerns of his own school.

At the end of the war with Germany in 1945, Lindeman was invited by the British Army to help with postwar German education. Gordon Hamilton, Lindeman's colleague, said that the events of this period bore out her impression that though he always wanted to be a realist, he was basically an idealist and was therefore liable to moments of disillusionment. These happened when social workers or churches failed to live up to the ideal he had sought for them. He had had no illusions about Nazi Germany and was well informed

[4] Memorandum from Lindeman to Mr. Pettit, September 14, 1942.

about it. Nevertheless, the situation he met in Germany was stagger-
ing. He was horrified when he saw the effects of indoctrination on
children and young people. He was terrified by the conceit, even
among the young, of belonging to the "master race." When the
British Army refused to allow him to do his educational work under
civilian control, he did not accept the long-range assignment. He
felt that the moral destruction of Germany was beyond all compre-
hension. He suggested that Germany be disarmed and that it should
be under control for a long time but that this control not be military.
He thought it futile to attempt to teach democracy to German adults.
One should concentrate instead on education in the schools as well
as in the youth services. In the following years both the American
and British High Commissioners carried through an intensive program of education of youth leaders. It is possible that this was partly
the result of Lindeman's recommendations.

The years after his return from Germany were filled with an
intensified inquiry into philosophical problems closely related to the
social scene in America, into the specific problems of civil liberties,
and into political issues. During this time many foreign visitors came
to the School and Lindeman developed close relations with them.
The School assumed an increasing responsibility for the work of
Americans in other countries and for the education of social workers
from foreign countries.

Lindeman's outside activities focused more intensely on the questions of civil liberties, child labor, and race relations. He was an
active member of the Commission of Inquiry into wartime treatment
of Negro servicemen of the Community Church of New York. His
interest in adult education was extended by his becoming a member
of the editorial staff of the New American Library of World Literature, on which he served until his death. In quick succession he
introduced inexpensive books, such as the ones of Emerson, *The
Basic Writings of America's Sage* (1947) and Max C. Otto, *Science
and the Moral Life* (1949). It was important to him that books be
available at a low price. Charlotte Demorest told how his own
library was always open to his students.

I developed the habit of pilfering from Lindeman. In his office on

22nd Street every square inch of space was jam-packed with books, pamphlets, papers, reprints, and scrapbooks. In spite of the efficient Miss Dekan's efforts, it resembled nothing so much as moving day at the library. You sometimes had to share twenty-four inches of chair with about sixteen inches of pamphlets. While killing time waiting for our conference, my eyes would wander over those piles of material that tempted me and other students sort of accidentally-on-purpose.

Frequently I lent him things too — at first thinking to get them back. Later after Miss Dekan had pursued some dozen students to their homes to recover some material lent-to-me-to-lend-to-Lindeman, I decided to grow up and rejoice when I saw my pet copy of Overstreet going down 22nd Street under the arm of a perfect stranger.[5]

Lindeman was also interested in the political events of the day; his notebooks, which he always kept carefully, are filled with clippings about the coming election of 1948 and with questions of means and ends in public policies. He took an open stand for Truman and the notes reveal his pleasure in the unexpected outcome of the election.

There were signs of oncoming illness. He never allowed ill health to interfere with his strenuous activities but in one of the 1948 notebooks we find a little note of a Minnesota highway sign which he copied: "Choose your rut carefully, you'll be in it for the next 25 miles" and next to it he had written, "I am tired and weary."

In 1949 he was invited to India to serve for three months as a visiting professor at the University of Delhi; Mrs. Lindeman accompanied him. He had prepared well for this trip by reading extensively about India. During the entire three months of travel he was quite ill, but he fulfilled his obligations. He was alive to new ideas. On the way, in Greece and in Egypt, he met many former students. In Africa he talked with Albert Schweitzer, who did not agree with Gandhi's fight for separation from Britain. Schweitzer said, according to Lindeman's notebook, "I had a great respect for Gandhi, but I never could understand why he did not foresee that the spirit of

[5] Charlotte K. Demorest, "He Saw the Mountain in the Molehill," *20th Anniversary Yearbook of Adult Education*, New York Education Council, 1953, p. 19.

nationalism which he had set in motion would not sooner or later become a worse evil than enlightened colonialism. He should never have led India away from the British Commonwealth."

Lindeman did not agree with this and he objected to the way the British had left the country. He was concerned about Indian nationalism and about the way indoctrination prevailed in India, but he felt that it was mainly Britain's colonial policies which had prevented wider educational opportunities. He understood that Indians had formerly derived their sense of security through the rigid caste system, through the power of the maharajas, and through their religion; he saw that the time had come when the Indian citizen had to change because his social system was changing. Even Gandhi's and Nehru's government seemed too authoritarian to Lindeman.

At the University of Delhi he employed his usual discussion method and ran into great difficulties with the students, who were accustomed to sitting at the feet of the teacher. In fact, he was once summoned by the president of the university for questioning about this method. Lindeman explained the reasons for his way of teaching and the president agreed to his continuing. Many Indian students kept up a correspondence with him after he returned to the United States.

While he was in India he was deeply impressed with the poverty around him. He felt that the United States as a rich country should take on the responsibility of economic and educational help. He came to respect the spiritual values he found in Indian life, and he began to read more about Oriental religions.

He studied Indian social work and especially their social work education. This he did with humility: while some other social work teachers went to foreign countries and began immediately to introduce American social work into the foreign setting, he first studied India's social institutions and social work efforts. He tried to understand the specific concepts and values underlying the different cultural patterns. In a report to the YWCA (he had taught at a YWCA college in India), he said,

Those skills which contribute to the operation of modern social welfare programs have, perhaps, been more highly developed in the

United States than elsewhere. This is not to infer that the American Welfare program is, in either its philosophy or its methods, superior to similar programs in other countries. It merely means that the technical aspects of social work have received more attention here. These skills should not, however, be directly transplanted in other cultures. The way in which technical knowledge and skill operates in differing cultures is not primarily a scientific or a technical matter. Each separate culture has its own history, its own continuities, and its own underlying concepts of value. Technics should not violate these cultural patterns. Technical skills, like visitors, need to be acclimatized.

Social work in India, and in the whole of Asia, stands at a different level than in the West. Its professionalization must make its own way in opposition to certain deep-seated and ancient conceptions. The act of helping a person in trouble is considered to be in Asiatic cultures, a personal equation. The thought of being paid a salary for helping others is to many repugnant. The empirical fact which reveals that those who strive to assist others often do much more harm than good is itself an accompaniment of technical and scientific experience and hence we should not expect to find it present in places where such experience has been scarce. When these facts are taken into consideration it becomes clear that American casework, group work, and community organization skills cannot be blandly taught nor applied in India. . . .

. . . The ends must belong to the Indian people. We may furnish some of the means, but the purposes and goals for which these instruments are to be used must be determined by Indian citizens. Otherwise, the effort to transplant skills will become a power instrument. This will happen no matter how generous our initial motives may be.[6]

When Lindeman returned from India at the beginning of 1950 to resume teaching at the New York School, he was concerned with the "climate" of the American scene. In the face of the climate produced by Senator McCarthy's investigations, he wondered what would happen to the courage of young people: he was afraid that the dissenter would no longer be accepted. Lindeman took a clear and unequivocal stand against Russia and Communist dogmatism; but just because of this clear stand, he was against restrictions on free

[6] Lindeman, "Pre-Point Four," *The Woman's Press*, September 1950, pp. 12–13.

thinking in this country. In the 1952 notebook we find quotes from Lincoln relevant to the current situation in the United States; for example, "It seems obvious to me that this nation was founded on the supposition that men have the right to protest, violently if need be, against authority that is unjust or oppressive." [7]

In 1950 Lindeman retired from the faculty of the New York School, and in a short essay in the *Survey* summarized his thoughts about retirement and his plans. He said in looking back, "The School has provided me with many opportunities for educational experiments . . . and best of all, has allowed me a wide scope of freedom." He talked about his plans for a second career. First he planned to teach undergraduates at the University of Kansas City, "a new kind of education for me." He wanted to continue his public lecturing: "I always learn something when I go out to talk with people." He wanted to continue reading — "the many books I haven't read yet."

He did not object to compulsory retirement, because it gave a man a chance to begin something new. Together with his friends Walter Pettit and Shelby M. Harrison, he planned a "senior consultation bureau" for welfare and educational institutions.

What was his view of the social work student and the social work problem at the time of his retirement? He thought the students were more specialized, more professionalized, more interested in a single aspect of social problems than they had been at the beginning of his career. There was, he said, a "greater tendency [for them] to fall into widely separated ideological camps."

He saw an increased "search for authority." He predicted an increase in public welfare work, and he hoped that volunteer welfare workers would come to be taken more seriously. He saw at this time as the most important landmarks in social work: (1) the fact that public welfare was accepted, (2) the expansion of social group work as a specialized field, (3) the increase of men in the profession of social work, (4) the introduction of casework into new areas, and (5) an increasing interest in labor and industry in the contribution of social work. At the end of this short summary he called himself

[7] Abraham Lincoln, Beardstown, August 12, 1858.

"the quasi-discouraged optimist."[8] He named civil liberties the most profound issue confronting the nation in 1950.

In spite of his increasingly bad health, he carried out most of his plans. He taught at Kansas City, he made a survey of the Pittsburgh YWCA, and he participated in the White House Conference on Children and Youth as a member of the National Committee.

The inexpensive Mentor Book Series published in 1951 Thomas Vernor Smith's and Eduard C. Lindeman's *The Democratic Way of Life*, which summarized Lindeman's thinking about applied values in a democracy.[9] In the introduction to the third printing in 1955, the publishers paid tribute to Lindeman as a "wise friend, teacher and philosopher."

In his notebooks he said, in 1952, "I am retired, I teach, I do research, I study history — being dedicated — work on urban redevelopment." One has the impression that this notation is almost jubilant because he felt he was capable of doing so much. In 1952 he was elected president of the National Conference of Social Work for 1953. His former student, Lester Granger, handed him the gavel. He appreciated this honor, but unfortunately it came so late that Lindeman never presided at the Conference.

Another honor came to him before his death. Colleagues and trustees of the School of Social Work decided to work on the establishment of a Lindeman Chair. They hoped that such a chair would continue the tradition of philosophy he had established. The gathering informing Lindeman of this honor was held in the house of Laura Pratt, one of the trustees of the New York School and a close friend of the Lindeman family. After this meeting Lindeman wrote a letter to Mrs. Pratt which shows how moved he was and sets forth his thinking in regard to the continuation of his life's work.

May I first of all express certain reflections regarding this business of retirement. One leads a very busy and active life for say fifty years and then suddenly it all comes to an end. Thereupon one moves into an unreal atmosphere, a fantastic world. You know then that you are living on borrowed time and each day seems inexpressibly

[8] *Survey*, October 1950, pp. 459–60.
[9] Thomas Vernor Smith and Eduard C. Lindeman, *The Democratic Way of Life* (New York: New American Library, 1951).

precious. And there are some days when it seems that life has already ended.

There is, for example, a sense of unreality about this occasion. I don't quite recognize this Eduard Lindeman you are talking about and for whom you propose to establish a professorial chair. He sounds like an interesting fellow and I hope some day to meet him. Incidentally, I must not allow all of this to induce conceit. Not at my age. In a recent reading of Emerson's Journals I came across a most interesting description of a conceited man. He was described by one of Emerson's friends as a man who had spent his entire adult life in the growing expectation that there might be a vacancy in the Trinity.

You have asked me to say something about the nature of the proposed Lindeman Chair in social philosophy. It would be easier to say what it ought not be. *It ought not be filled by someone who attempts an imitation of Lindeman.* He must be a creative person in his own right. I can imagine this person spending at least a half-year at the New York School of Social Work without doing any teaching. I can imagine him "tasting" the School, its students, its faculty, its graduates and its trustees and gradually formulating some outlines of courses. I can then see him submitting these course outlines to the Curriculum Committee and I can then see him gradually putting these new courses into experimental use. *He must not be an ivory tower Philosopher but rather one who plays an active role in the life of the community, the nation and the world. He must not be dogmatic or doctrinaire. He should be willing to test his principles by putting these to the test in active affairs. And, if I were to advise this young person further, I think I would suggest that he dedicate himself to the task of bringing social work into a realistic alignment with religion and ethics.*

But I must stop, but not without expressing my gratitude to this company of friends who have undertaken the task of establishing the Lindeman Chair in social philosophy at the New York School of Social Work where most of my professional life was spent. As I said earlier, it all seems unreal and your generous spirit has left me slightly tongue-tied. My gratitude comes from the heart.[10]

The election to the presidency of the National Conference of Social Work meant increased work and traveling. Lindeman also was in great demand for lectures. During these activities, in 1952 and 1953, he was very sick. He suffered from uremia, a severe and

---

[10] Lindeman, letter to Laura Pratt, February 1, 1953, italics mine.

fatal disease of the kidneys; he also had heart damage. Mrs. Linde-man described his intense suffering on his returning from giving speeches.

Walter Pettit remembered that in the winter of 1952 Lindeman was so sick he could not sleep lying down. Yet, after a night spent in a chair in a hotel room the two shared when they made agency surveys in cities outside of New York, Lindeman would get up and conduct meetings and speak, without letting others know of his suffering.

He went reluctantly to the hospital for his last stay, saying quietly to his wife, "I won't come back." While he was in the hospital friends wrote and visited him, everybody expecting him to continue his active life. On his last day he had his family around him. He said to them, "This is a beautiful country. Don't let McCarthy spoil it! It is up to you, the younger generation, now to do your part. America is good. Keep it good."

Eduard C. Lindeman died April 13, 1953. The letters that came to the family manifested the esteem in which he was held over the entire world. Almost all of them expressed the belief that his ideas and ideals would remain alive.

Let me summarize Lindeman's personality in the words of three of his friends: Roger Baldwin, the fighter for civil liberties; his former student Lester B. Granger, educator and community worker for the improvement of race relations; and Laura Pratt, the family friend and the volunteer in social work with a deep understanding of its many-fold tasks.

In a memo written not as an obituary but spontaneously, when I asked for an interview, Roger Baldwin said:

It did not take long before I first met Ed Lindeman in New York in the early 1920's for us to become intimate friends. We were of about the same age; we were both in the liberal camp; we shared the same values with the same sense of humor about them; we didn't take ourselves too seriously, and we both had a spirit of fun. . . .

I heard him speak to large audiences and saw his power of quiet persuasion through the clarity and simplicity of his utterance, his intensity of expression and his appeal to lofty sentiments. He had no tricks of oratory — tho mannerisms, of course — but he infused speech with repressed emotion which carried his hearers right along with him. His private speech reflected the same quiet emotional quality, backed by obvious deliberation. His students, so they told me, found him the most challenging and arresting teacher in the school. He posed problems which he made them answer, often dividing his classes into "left" and "right" and getting them to debate an issue, one against the other.

Even on matters on which I know he had deep convictions I never found him dogmatic. He was as tolerant of all opinion as he was modest in voicing his own. We were not agreed on pacifism, but he never questioned mine. He did not, like me, see with such hope the democratic claims of Communism and the Soviet Union, but he conceded I might be right, and when I was proved wrong, never recalled my earlier illusions. I do not recollect over all the years a single argument. He did not argue; he stated his views and let them go for what they were worth. Even in the hot debates of the Civil Liberties Union Board, he rarely spoke up, but he always voted on the more liberal, — that is, the less cautious, — side. He held no grudges; he took no part in factions; if he was critical he voiced his dissent in kindly and temperate words. I never heard him express hate of anybody; his attitudes were impersonal, and while he condemned many evils he did not condemn persons. Of one garrulous woman I could only gather his dislike by his asking me if I found her "conversation interesting."

. . . He sensed the human side of any situation with sympathy, he was compassionate even with those he thought had done wrong. He was always relaxed, present with his whole self, diverted neither by the past nor worried over what might come.

Ed did not shy away from any idea or movement because it was unpopular or dangerous. He did not recognize "dangerous thoughts," nor people nor movements. He was a radical in the actual sense of the word, but he held to no isms. He wore no labels, but he was curious enough to examine and appraise all who did. Even his identification with the New Deal made him no thick-and-thin New Dealer. His long identification with social work made him no apologist for its limitations. He always stressed the added need for social action, and practiced it in his many activities. It was in that field of action rather than in his philosophy or teaching that he and I shared our major interests.

He enjoyed everything he did, richly and fully, from his reading, teaching, speaking — his major concerns — to ballgames, social life, tennis, bird-watching and his family. While he was involved deeply in trying to understand and interpret the society in which he lived, he was at heart a heretic. He could not reconcile that society with the human values he stressed. No acquisitive civilization could meet his ideals; no nationalism; no wars; no racism. Yet heretic as he was to the status quo, he was no revolutionist nor even far on the left of reform. He was no fighter; no controversialist. Some good causes promoted by Communists caught him unawares, to his later discomfort, but he had no conscious identification with the left. He worked where practical results seemed possible in immediate specific reforms — civil liberties, child labor, Indians' rights, adult education, industrial democracy, academic freedom.

I know less of his philosophy, but in the larger frame of social thinking and relations, I always placed him with the school he came most to admire — the Concord of Emerson, Thoreau and Alcott. If he was an apostle of John Dewey in philosophic method he was a disciple in spirit of the Concord dissenters who challenged all conformity.

It always struck me as a bit incongruous that a teacher with these nonconformist ideals should be a professor in a social work school whose professional techniques and outlook are so conformist. But I counted it a tribute to the profession that it could recognize Lindeman as one of them; one whom indeed it needed if its vision were to be raised beyond the maladjustments of a competitive society to the high levels of man's capacity for fraternity, equality and justice.

Lester Granger spoke at the memorial services.

When I had word of the serious illness and expected death of Eduard Lindeman I had just returned to my office from a three weeks' absence. I was sitting in my office on a very cold and rainy Sunday afternoon reading accumulated correspondence and I came upon the advance announcement. I called our friend, Tom Cotton, who confirmed my worst suspicions, and I looked out and the outside was darker and something of the darkness came into the room.

I am not ashamed to say that I sat there and wept a bit, because I loved the man. I should not have trusted myself to talk today, because I find that philosophical reassurances as to the deathlessness of the human personality does not necessarily heal the hurt that we feel when a loved one has passed. But it is true — and we know this is true and we must never let it be denied — that it is impossible for a good man really to die. Because such a man lives on as long as his influence — as long as his example manifested in the beliefs and practices of his followers.

In this sense Eduard Lindeman will never die, because the examples that he set in education and social practice and social action, and the wisdom he shared with his colleagues and with generations of workers in training, made so deep an impression on professional practice and professional concept as to make it impossible for his influence ever to fade away. The foundations of a building may be covered up, but as long as the building stands we know that the foundation is there, securely supported and ruggedly dependable. And Eduard Lindeman is in so many ways the foundation of what is still being erected in social work practice and development, and in the development of adult education that it would be impossible to carry on further developments in these fields without depending upon and frequently referring to the fundaments established by this pioneer in the modern science of better social living.

. . . What set him apart from other interpreters of professional method was the amount of personal conviction, of glowing faith, which he constantly infused into his subject. More than any other one person, Ed Lindeman was responsible during the past quarter century for what has amounted to a complete revolution in the social philosophy of staff and board members of thousands of social agencies throughout the country. He taught the field of adult education that education of any sort is not the enforcement of learning upon people, but is the sharing of wisdom between teacher and student.

He accomplished his revolution by constant reference to and lucid interpretation of the democratic concept as it relates to education and social work. He was a man who had no patience with dogma, whether that dogma be presented with a liberal or conservative label. He always insisted that dogmas are the refuge of the sensitive, — the over-sensitive and frustrated who cannot endure to face realities — or sanctions to persecutions and brutality for the insensitive and unscrupulous. And Dr. Lindeman insisted that democracy demands a constantly fluid, and not a static set of values, and that only the strong — the strong of heart and the tough of spirit — are able to maintain faith in the democratic method under current grinding social pressures.

Laura Pratt wrote on April 8, 1953, a few days before Lindeman's death:

Friendship has an ever-widening arc. . . . life has brought a close sense of friendship through Eduard C. Lindeman that is all of ours to keep. I cannot quite remember the date, but I do remember the time when Eduard Lindeman looked at me concentratedly, directly, and raised a question. I recalled my hesitancy to assume a responsibility which was obviously the next step. Then his kindness and kind of urging and pulling and opening up possibilities. Through these ten years that is exactly what he has done to many of us. He certainly fortified Charlotte Demorest and myself . . . because he had helped us to learn the importance of laying open ideas on which people would snare themselves, on laying the best of plans with which people could work, and always holding to an open-minded and open-hearted atmosphere. These friendship groups are a Lindeman natural, patterns for our lives, and making a real contribution toward human understanding. . . . This whole Plan [for a Lindeman Chair] will be on-going in the field of social work, in human relations, far outlasting all of our spans of human life. That is what greatness creates.

These hopes that Lindeman's ideas and ideals will remain alive justify the last notation in his notebook, which oddly enough summarizes Lindeman's outlook on life though he did not realize that death was imminent:

Immediate outlook — pessimistic. Long view — optimistic.

PART TWO

The Development of a Philosophy

"THE conflicts of our world are not simply conflicts of practical interests. They also represent conflicts of ideas and ideals." Charles A. Ellwood, *A History of Social Philosophy*, p. 554.

CHAPTER 5

SOCIAL WORK'S GOALS AND VALUES IN HISTORICAL PERSPECTIVE

To UNDERSTAND the place of Eduard Lindeman's thinking in social work we must first examine the development of values and goals in the profession itself. In this chapter the historical development of social work will be traced with the primary focus on its value component up to the time Lindeman entered the profession.

Social work, concerned with human relations and the solving of certain human problems, is almost as wide as life itself, and the development of its philosophy cannot be separated from the development of philosophical thought in all other human institutions in each country where it grew. This study will limit itself to the development in organized social work in the United States of America as it is expressed in the fairly limited number of writings consciously directed toward development of a philosophy. Social work is an entity representing three clearly distinguished but interrelated parts: a network of social services, carefully developed methods and processes, and social policy expressed through social institutions and individuals. All three are based on a view of human beings, their interrelationships, and the ethical demands made on them.

What is philosophy? The word is often used interchangeably with "theory" and their meanings are closely related. Yet they should be distinguished for purposes of clarity. Until the nineteenth century, philosophy comprised the thinking of all disciplines, and was divided into natural philosophy (which is now physics and other natural sciences) and mental and moral philosophy (which is now psychology, social science, and ethics). According to Webster's New International Dictionary philosophy is "The science which investigates the most general facts and principles of reality and human nature and conduct: specifically, and now usually, the science which comprises logic, ethics, esthetics, metaphysics and the theory of knowledge." Webster also states that in general, philosophy is more concerned with evaluation than with description; John Dewey affirms this: "It is concerned with problems of being and occurrence from the standpoint of value, rather than from that of mere existence." [1]

It is in this latter sense that the word philosophy is used here. Without question, values and ethical relationships cannot be considered without a theory of man, society, and nature. Yet philosophy is distinct from theory. Webster's Dictionary gives seven different definitions of the word "theory." The one selected is "A general principle, formula or ideal construction offered to explain phenomena and rendered more or less plausible by evidence in the facts or by the exactness and relevancy of the reasoning." Theory, therefore, will mainly contain the discoveries or hypotheses regarding what *is*; philosophy, while based partly on theory, will include what *should be*.

This study is concerned with the value and goal orientation of social work. From its beginning social work has been based on certain assumptions about man and society (theory) and their moral obligations to each other (philosophy). It is significant that the title of a lecture given in 1900 by Frances G. Peabody at Harvard University, which inspired many young men to enter social work, was "The Ethics of Social Reform. The Questions of Charity, Divorce, the Indians, Labor, Prisons, Temperance, etc. as Problems of Practical Ethics . . ." [2] The title indicated that social work was more "practical ethics" than, as was said in later years, "applied social sciences." This change of emphasis indicates social work's constant struggle to reconcile a scientific base with ethical demands.

Social work's earliest function was to give material aid. This was closely related to religious motivation. As long as societies were

[1] John Dewey, *Philosophy, Encyclopedia of the Social Sciences* (New York: Macmillan, April 1935), p. 122.

[2] Frank J. Bruno, *Trends in Social Work* (New York: Columbia University Press, 1938), p. 133.

predominantly theocratic states, the function of helping the poor was given to the church or to other religious organizations. The Jewish tradition held that the poor are God's wards and pensioners, and that God, as a God of justice, demands that restitution be made to the poor for what they have been deprived of. God as a God of compassion also asked for sympathy for the poor.

The Jewish group was not only a religious group but it was also a community. During centuries of persecution the Jews had learned that anybody might become poor and need help. Their philosophy of giving grew out of a basic feeling of responsibility for a suffering neighbor and it always put great stress on the importance of not shaming him and of considering him as an equal. It was the custom at some high holidays — for example at the festival of Passover — to receive some of the poor in one's own home and have them as guests at the family table without making any distinction between them and any other guest of the family.

These strong feelings of responsibility for the neighbor and respect for his feelings were expressed by the philosopher Maimonides in his classification of the eight different kinds of donor:

1. He who gives grudgingly, reluctantly or with regret.
2. He who gives less than he should, but gives graciously.
3. He who gives what he should, but only after he is asked.
4. He who gives before he is asked.
5. He who gives without knowing to whom he gives although the recipient knows the identity of the donor.
6. He who gives without making his identity known.
7. He who gives without knowing to whom he gives, neither does the recipient know from whom he receives.
8. He who helps a fellowman to support himself by a gift or a loan or by finding employment for him, thus helping him to become self-supporting.[3]

The last was considered the highest form of giving since it respected the dignity of the poor and brought them back into the community as self-respecting members.

The Christian philosophy of charity had the same root but added

---

[3] "Matnot Aniyim," Chapter 10, verses 7–13, *Sabbath and Festival Prayerbook*, published by the United Synagogues of America.

to it the example of Jesus. It was based on Matthew 25:35–40: "for I was hungry and you gave me to eat; I was thirsty and you gave me to drink; I was a stranger and you took me in; naked and you covered me; sick and you visited me; I was in prison and you came unto me. . . . I say to you as long as you did it to one of these my least brethren, you did it to me." It also considered the poor the brothers of the rich — as not really different from everybody else; persecution had taught this to the early Christian community.

Yet with the rise of the church as a worldly power, the philosophy changed subtly. The poor became people to be helped because of Christ's example, but they were somewhat set apart from the rest of the population. And with the rise of Protestantism yet another subtle change in the approach to giving occurred. While the Catholic Church considered giving one of the ways in which man worked on his salvation during his lifetime, Protestantism did not consider good works as requisite to salvation but rather it considered faith all-important. Man need not be good to be saved, although he had originally been saved by Christ and therefore had an obligation to be good. This theological difference influenced the change in the attitude toward charity. Protestants encouraged the state to take responsibility for the poor.

With this development the attitudes toward giving and toward the person to be supported were also changing. Depending on their stage of political development, societies to some degree developed services to the poor as a community responsibility (as in the early settlements in the United States). They considered such services the responsibility of the owner of property — as in feudal society or in the system of slavery, or the state's responsibility because of the nuisance the poor presented — as expressed in the Elizabethan Poor Laws. The combination of giving and punishing was not an outgrowth of church teaching, though it was often supported by churches which were closely identified with the worldly power. If the early settlers in the United States had been completely unrelated to and uninfluenced by the developments and thinking in their country of origin, social work philosophy could have developed on a much more democratic basis.

The development of community responsibility in the political area came early in the United States. The Declaration of Independence, in stating "that all men are created equal, that they are endowed by their Creator with certain inalienable Rights, that among these are Life, Liberty and the pursuit of Happiness," clearly established the basic philosophy of respect for all people regardless of race, creed, color — or economic status. A study of the development of the philosophy of services to the needy shows, however, that acceptance of this idea was slow, and it is not fully accepted even today.

While the Declaration, based on religious and humanistic philosophy, stressed the *right* to "Life, Liberty and the pursuit of Happiness," actual social services continued to be restrictive. The early history of social work is full of considerations, for instance, of whether a poor person is "worthy" or not, whether help should be given to those who are not "valuable" to society. Poverty was treated as complete dependency, with the poor having no say in decision-making, with their activities supervised and their domiciles determined. A good example of this is the giving of relief "in kind" instead of in money; for a long time the poor were not considered capable of determining their own needs and of budgeting their own money. Services to people with other problems — to dependent children, unmarried mothers, lawbreakers, and the mentally sick — were all handled with the same basic convictions that people with difficulties were different from those who did not have them, and that the essential difference lay in their incapacity to handle their own affairs. This basic philosophy was usually supported by current scientific theories.

In the seventeenth and eighteenth centuries, poverty was usually attributed to laziness and drunkenness, thus making the individual wholly responsible for his economic status. In the beginning of the twentieth century a change occurred because of the interest in psychological testing and the emphasis on environmental factors as causes for differing behavior. The poor man was no more considered wholly responsible for his fate. His condition was seen as a result of mental retardation or unfavorable environment. The discovery of such new factors changed the practice of social work.

It was at this time — around the end of the nineteenth century and beginning of the twentieth — that the influence of the Elizabethan Poor Laws began to wane. And it is of this time that we can say that it saw the beginning of an organized development of the social work profession in the United States.

Many basic changes in the environment had an impact on the philosophy of giving.

During the middle part of the nineteenth century immigration increased and with it industrialization. Funds for public charity were meager, and were supplemented by private charity. The first Charity Organization Society was founded in Buffalo in 1877. This society, and those that were created after it, followed the example set in England where the first Charity Organization Society was organized in 1869. These in turn had their forerunners in the charity organizations in Elberfeld and Hamburg, Germany, which used the friendly visitors to individualize services and to investigate needs. The Charity Organization Society movement had the greatest influence on social work as a growing profession through its practice and writing (Amos Warner in Baltimore and Mary Richmond in Baltimore and New York), its research efforts (the charity organization department of the Russell Sage Foundation in New York, founded in 1909), and its beginning of the first professional school (the summer school of philanthropy in New York in 1898).

The period between 1890 and the First World War was the era of American reform movements. Samuel Morison and Henry Steele Commager describe the period:

Its manifestations . . . agrarian revolt . . . strong government regulation over industry . . . new and intelligent concern for the poor and the underprivileged, for women and children, for the victims and derelicts of society, for the immigrant, the Indian and the Negro . . . reform of political machinery . . . restoration of business ethics . . . a new social and political philosophy, a philosophy that rejected laissez faire and justified public control of social and economic institutions on the principles of liberal democracy.[4]

[4] Samuel E. Morison and Henry S. Commager, *The Growth of the American Republic*, II (New York: Oxford University Press, 1942), p. 356.

Many of these reforms were of direct concern to social workers. The movements that had a lasting influence on social work — even though it was less apparent for a period of time, especially between 1915 and the beginning of the depression — were the settlement house movement, the movement to create agencies to serve youth, and the movement for reform of correctional institutions.

The settlement house movement was strongly influenced by English practice. In 1884 Toynbee Hall was founded in London and in 1886 followed the first settlement house in the United States, Neighborhood Guild in New York. The original purpose of the settlement houses was to acquaint students with the life of laborers and the poor by enabling students to live among them. The first residents of settlement houses were driven by a strong sense of justice. In the United States another purpose was added almost immediately: to acquaint students with the new immigrant, his culture, and his needs, and thereby help them to integrate the immigrant into the new country. The insights gained by these residents led quickly to action and the settlements became the centers of direct service and reform. The residents helped the individual neighbor who came to them with filling out papers, learning the new language, and taking care of the baby; they also offered him a place to relax and get away from crowded living quarters. They collected data about living conditions in the slums and brought to the attention of the legislature unsanitary conditions, misuse of child labor, and the effect of wages that were far too low.

They recognized it as their task not only to fight the usual causes of breakdown — poverty and delinquency, for instance — but also the threats to the basis of democracy that lie in ignorance and in discrimination against any part of the population. Robert A. Woods, the head resident of one of the earliest settlement houses, South End House of Boston, describes this goal: "The social worker thus serves to unite the new scattered industrial, racial and religious elements that are thrown together to make up the population particularly of our great city communities." [5] The settlement houses became living

[5] Robert A. Woods, *The Neighborhood in Nation Building* (Boston: Houghton, 1923), p. 94.

training grounds where different groups learned to live together and understand each other.

The settlement movement also contributed to the change of attitude toward the poor away from what had been implied in the Poor Laws. Jane Addams — speaking from her experience at Hull House in Chicago — said to the National Conference in 1897: "I have not the great fear of pauperizing people which many of you seem to have. We have all accepted bread from someone, at least until we were fourteen . . . If we can only make the medium of giving friendly enough . . . it does not make any difference whether you give an old Latin Grammar or a pair of shoes." [6] And "The settlement, accurately speaking, stands not for relief, nor for instruction, but for fellowship." [7]

Both Jane Addams and Robert Woods, and with them the settlement house movement, treated the poor as fellow human beings, an attitude of respect on which modern social work is based. The value of *equality* between the giver and the one who had to take, and the value of *cultural pluralism* — the recognition of the right to be different and yet equal — entered social work's thinking largely by way of the settlement movement.

Another influence pulling social work away from the "Lady Bountiful" attitude came from the agencies or movements serving youth and young adults. In 1851 the YMCA (Young Men's Christian Association) was founded in Boston and in 1866 the YWCA (Young Women's Christian Association) was begun. After 1900 other organizations such as the YMWHA (Young Men and Women's Hebrew Association), the CYO (Catholic Youth Organization), the Boy Scouts, Girl Scouts, and Campfire Girls came into being. They had their bases in the health, recreational, educational, and cultural needs of young people and included also the "tendency to organize for social ends" and "to take part in public concerns through voluntary organization." [8] These organizations directed their efforts toward all youth, whether economically deprived or not, thus antici-

[6] Bruno, *op. cit.*, p. 114.
[7] Woods, *op. cit.*, p. 52.
[8] Grace L. Coyle, *Group Work with American Youth* (New York: Harper, 1948), p. 3.

pating a later trend of social work and stressing a philosophy of "equal opportunity, mutual dependence," and "self-help." The International Institutes of the YWCA were pioneers in appreciating the culture of the foreign-born and helping him to integrate without forcing him to abandon what was valuable to him. The Industrial Department of the same organization was the strongest link social work had with the rising labor movement.

Significant reforms were also carried out in the correctional field, which was close to general social work during the period of the reform movements. Frederick Wines, one of the founders of the National Conference of Charities and Corrections, combined his interest in charity with an interest in the correction field. He was appointed the first secretary of the state board of correction of Illinois. His father, Enoch C. Wines, was secretary of the New York Prison Association and very active in prison reform. In 1899 the first juvenile court was created in Chicago and in 1909 Dr. William Healy called a psychiatric social worker to the court, more in a clinical capacity than for direct court work. Probation and parole work were not generally done by social workers until recently. Prison and court reforms showed the increasing influence on social institutions of humanitarian thinking. The mental health movement, brought to life by the courageous book by Clifford Beers, *A Mind that Found Himself*, found strong support in such people as William James.

The twentieth century also became known as the "Century of the Child," so named after Ellen Key's book. The interest in the child was closely related to the new "enlightenment" of the twentieth century. The eighteenth century, with Voltaire, Rousseau, and Jefferson, had pronounced the great humanitarian ideas, and the implementation of these ideas on the political scene had begun; but the ideas had not yet entered the lives of individuals and small groups. Rousseau could preach humanitarianism and then place his children in foundling homes without people considering this a violation of his principles.

The twentieth century began to demand the application of humanitarian ideals on all fronts: in political and economic organizations, in neighborhood work with various national and racial groups, in general youth organizations, in prisons and mental hospitals. No wonder that the reawakened sense of justice turned also toward the most helpless member of society, the child. While homeless children had been cared for for centuries, they had been looked upon as commodities. A child could be removed from a family like a piece of furniture without being asked himself, and even without the permission of those close to him. And a child in his own family was the property of the parents, without rights and without legal protection. The growing understanding offered by psychology showed that the child could think for himself, and that he was neither a miniature adult nor a dumb lump of flesh. He was a unique personality. And he was the most dependent personality in society.

The right to make decisions began to be extended to children and their families and protection of such rights by law began to take shape in the children's field. The first White House Conference on Children and Youth was called in 1909. Its major recommendation meant a revolution in social work: no child should be removed from his family solely for economic reasons. This also brought the beginning of aid in their own homes for mothers with dependent children instead of the earlier practice of placing the children in institutions. The need for such aid was immense because of the high incidence of deaths of fathers from work accidents and industrial diseases. This recommendation put another dent in the punitive attitude of the Poor Laws. In 1912 the Children's Bureau was founded, making the welfare of children a federal responsibility, though certainly not exclusively a federal one.

The early years of the twentieth century were the years of the struggle of the young social work profession to clarify its goals, establish itself as an entity, and develop a common body of knowledge teachable in its own schools. All these endeavors were interrelated. But the struggle toward the goals — goals often not clearly enunciated, but always present — determined practice.

The presidential address of the Conference of Charities and Corrections in 1900 stressed not only the goal of healing but the goal of *prevention.*

Let us remember that the charity which prevents human suffering is kinder than the charity which relieves it, and that, while the noble institutions created by society for the benefit of its weaker members are testimonials to benevolence and wise statesmanship, they are in a larger sense the sad witnesses of the neglect of the wiser charity, which would, in the fulfillment of God's purpose, render their existence unnecessary.[9]

Thinking of people as *individuals* rather than as masses was considered by some as in contrast with the attitude of the reformer. Frederick Wines looked upon the reformer as a zealous person with no knowledge and too little love. His philosophy, stressing the need for the friendly visitor and the individual approach, rested on a strongly religious base: he believed that "healing comes by the touch, that men are saved not in masses, but one by one, and that everyone saved must be saved by an individual whose own heart is filled with love, and who is able to communicate to another the grace which he himself has received."[10]

But this warm interest in the individual stood side by side at the conference with the concept of the poor person as being guilty for his situation.

No system should encourage improvidence by giving to the unthrifty at every crisis of their lives advantages for which the thrifty have toiled and economized. . . . The improvident and reckless should, of course, be relieved, adequately and humanely, but on conditions distinctly and avowedly unattractive.[11]

The acceptance by society of the disadvantaged as simply a human being in need is not easily brought about. However, social work's leadership drove toward it. The dominating concepts in those early years were *individualization* and *the friendly visitor*. Individualization applied not only to the charity organization worker, but showed

---

[9] Charles E. Faulkner, *Proceedings*, National Conference of Charities and Corrections, 27th Annual Session, Topeka, Kans. (Boston: George H. Ellis, 1900), p. 2.

[10] Frederick H. Wines, "The Healing Touch," *Proceedings*, National Conference of Charities and Corrections, 27th Annual Session, Topeka, Kans. (Boston: George H. Ellis, 1900), p. 25.

[11] Hugh F. Fox, "Centralizing Tendencies in Administration," *Proceedings*, National Conference of Charities and Corrections, 27th Annual Session, Topeka, Kans. (Boston: George H. Ellis, 1900), p. 134.

up in many other areas of social work. "The division of the large boys' club into small groups, the abandonment of the barrack method in homes and hospitals and reformatories, and the creating of new institutions with many small houses instead of one big one, illustrate the present tendency." [12]

In discussions of the friendly visitor the emphasis was placed on doing away with *a cold, distant attitude* and on bringing about *cooperation* with the client or the group. This emphasis showed value change in the profession. Jacob A. Riis in his beautiful speech "A Blast of Cheer" stressed the environmental influence on a "bad boy's" development. Talking about the settlement as a bridge between the helper and the one who needs help, he said,

We have brought common sense into the partnership to keep it from becoming a fad, human hearts to keep it from becoming a mere laboratory for social inquiry. Preserve me from the term "laboratory work." A human being in misery is not a bug to be stuck upon a pin for leisurely investigation and learned indexing. [13]

And Mary Richmond said,

We have all been the victims of the official who protects himself by a highly impersonal manner; and even when we have understood, we have been offended. The poor, who do not understand, are doubly offended, when the charity worker's attitude is impersonal. . . .

From the charity worker who reported on a family "Nothing unfavorable; gave 50 cts." up to the best modern type of professional worker, who particularly strives to develop by cooperation, all possibilities of help within and without the family, is a far cry. [14]

This emphasis on cooperation with client and group increased. The early years saw the beginning of schools of social work, as described in the preceding chapter. A method of work began to develop. The expression "casework" was probably first used by C. F.

[12] Rev. George Hodges, D.D., "The Progress of Compassion," *Proceedings*, National Conference of Charities and Corrections, 27th Annual Session, Topeka, Kans. (Boston: George H. Ellis, 1900), p. 10.

[13] Jacob A. Riis, "A Blast of Cheer," *Proceedings*, National Conference of Charities and Corrections, 27th Annual Session, Topeka, Kans. (Boston: George H. Ellis, 1900), p. 24.

[14] Mary Richmond, "Charitable Cooperation," *Proceedings*, National Conference of Charities and Corrections, 27th Annual Session, Topeka, Kans. (Boston: George H. Ellis, 1900), pp. 302, 306.

Weller of the Charity Organization Society (COS) in Washington in 1902. He meant by it the careful study of a case, including both the individual and the social approach.

. . . case study is not exclusively individual. To master cases we must also study neighborhoods and community life. . . . "Society," "Social relations," "Social Service" — these are the words we must repeat and emphasize to correct the conservative tendencies which would over-estimate individualism, consider only the individual causes of distress, and be content merely with individual casework.

He went further than suggesting the friendly visitor when he talked about the organization of clubs — "of so organizing comparatively resourceless people themselves that they shall stimulate, develop and assist each other." [15]

Social work in those years was not separated according to methods. Social workers disagreed on questions of mass reform or individualized approach, on the relative importance of private initiative and public responsibility, on explanations of poverty and disease, but not on the importance of different individualized approaches. The friendly visitor and the social worker with the small group belonged together. Nor were they separated on the basis of the kind of help they gave. The Conference Proceedings showed an equal concern for economic aid to widows, cultural provisions for newcomers, recreation for the children in the growing industrial centers, child labor, and the provision of nursery schools.

Seen from the vantage point of today, social work in the years before the First World War was a diversified but not a disunited profession. Its major struggle was to learn how to work *with* people, not *for* people. It moved from a value of *charity* in the narrow sense of giving by one "above" to one "below," toward the value of *justice* or equal opportunities.[16] The Owen R. Lovejoy report was a culmination of this development. It spelled out the rights of the disadvantaged; it demanded a living wage, an eight-hour working day, safety

[15] C. F. Weller, "Relief Work and Preventive Philanthropies," *Proceedings*, National Conference of Charities and Corrections, 29th Annual Session, Detroit, May 28–June 3, 1902, Isabel C. Barron, ed. (Boston: George H. Ellis, 1902), pp. 272, 275.

[16] Owen R. Lovejoy, *Proceedings*, National Conference of Charities and Corrections, 1912, pp. 376–94.

and health measures for workers, laws against child labor, a decent home, and social insurance.

The editor who introduced the *Proceedings* of the National Conference of 1913 said: "Nothing could show more clearly the passing of the old *charity* ideal and the coming in of the *social justice* ideal that has supplanted it than the proceedings of the 40th Conference (p. iii)."

In the years that followed this conference, there was a growing interest in preparing competent professional workers to put the social justice approach into practice. This interest was manifest in several areas. (1) The *family service* growing out of the COS efforts made stronger the individual approach which was strongly supported by the new influence of psychoanalysis. (2) Increased *club work* aimed at educating people to responsible citizenship. (3) The 1914 *Proceedings* show great emphasis on *recreation*, not as entertainment, but as the medium of learning self-government, of awakening latent cultural resources, and of preventing social ills.[17]

The profession presented a picture of balance between the individual and the group approach, a healthy investigation of scientific knowledge which could help it to achieve its task (knowledge derived mainly from sociology and psychiatry), a spread over many fields with a strong emphasis on the value of social justice. Casework method began to develop. The group work method was used, but little investigated.

In 1915 Abraham Flexner spoke at the National Conference on the question, "Is Social Work a Profession?" This is generally considered an important milestone in the history of social work because it introduced a more self-conscious preoccupation with social work method. If this led to *excessive* preoccupation with method, that certainly was not Flexner's intention. His speech was a thoughtful analysis of the state of social work in 1915 compared with objective standards for a profession. He emphasized that professional standing did not consist only in prestige or academic degrees. Rather, he said,

---

[17] See quote from Jane Addams in George A. Bellamy, "Recreation and Social Progress; The Settlement," *Proceedings*, National Conference of Charities and Corrections, 1914, p. 377.

a profession (1) is based mainly on an intellectual process; (2) requires personal responsibility in contrast to a job that is merely routine or involves only technique; (3) has a learned character and puts ideas into practice; (4) must be practical, have clearly defined ends, and develop "a technique capable of communication through an orderly and highly specialized educational discipline"; (5) must be a brotherhood which is distinct in its responsibility toward those it serves: "professional activities are so definite, so absorbent in interest, so rich in duties and responsibilities, that they completely engage their votaries"; (6) includes workers engaged in advancing common interests.

After having set these standards, Flexner compared them with the status of social work at the time and found that the profession already fulfilled several of his criteria. But it did not meet some of them, especially the one requiring a technique capable of communication. He also wondered whether social work had too wide a scope and perhaps was more "an aspect of work in many fields." With great modesty Flexner said that he was not sure whether social work might not develop in these areas, too, and all he wanted to say was that social work should know its limitations as well as its strengths.[18]

It was perhaps more Frank Bruno's interpretation of the Flexner speech than the speech itself which made many social workers ascribe to it the responsibility for the extraordinary interest in technique which followed. It is obvious in reading the full speech that this interpretation is misleading. I had the privilege of interviewing Dr. Flexner (who at the time was 88 years old) in 1955. He stressed that the development of a communicable technique was only *one* criterion. He emphasized again that if a profession considers technique alone without goals and good will and humanitarian intentions it "loses its heart" and is no profession. In this interview he enlarged on this, and cautioned vigorously against too much rigidity in standards. He reminded me of his role in standardizing medical

[18] Abraham Flexner, "Is Social Work a Profession?", *Proceedings*, National Conference of Charities and Corrections (Baltimore, Md., 1915), pp. 580, 585.

education in the United States but said that standardization should not prevent professions from being flexible where flexibility was indicated. He said, "The first great rule is that rules can be broken." He did not pretend that he had kept up with the development of social work, but said that in 1955 as in 1915 he had high regard for the humanitarian aims of social work and would consider it unfortunate if his criterion of technique had overshadowed every other consideration.

Only two years after Flexner's speech Mary Richmond's *Social Diagnosis* appeared, opening the era of intense preoccupation with method in social work. This was hardly her intent. She expected a greater scientific discipline of social workers; she demanded high individualization and orderly procedure in investigation and helping. She did not leave out consideration of environment or the value of compassion.

Mary Richmond did not like "reformers" and she often resisted legislative action — as, for example, in her fight against one of the first kinds of social insurance, widows' pensions — but not as a matter of principle. Much of her book coincided with the thinking implicit in the increased use of psychiatric techniques during World War I.

The insights gained from psychoanalysis during World War I had a profound influence on social work. Casework reached out for the psychiatric knowledge, because it supplied an additional tool for understanding the individual client, and it gave the social worker a more accepting and nonjudgmental attitude. This enriching development also had its disadvantage: it pushed social work too far into the treatment area and drew a part of its attention away from social conditions and reform.

This trend was probably intensified by the general atmosphere of the boom years after World War I. Reaction against the idealistic impetus for entering the war had set in. On the political scene there was a withdrawal from social responsibility — as seen, for example, in the refusal of the United States to join the League of Nations. Concern with self was far greater than concern with social conditions.

Individuals *were* troubled and there were real reasons for psychological upheaval. Women's changing place in society was probably the greatest revolution in centuries and surely the most far-reaching one, since it affected the primary group, the family, the base of society. This revolution was not just a reversal of roles (as in some matriarchal societies and as the comic strips like to present it); it meant a completely new family constellation. It raised the questions of democratic human relations, of freedom and limitation, of equality and its deeper meaning — right at the core of our most important institution. It changed the relation of parents to children and children to parents. It opened the question of education for whom and for what. It changed the composition of the labor market. No wonder that the inner conflicts of people were important. Whenever societies undergo major cultural changes individuals will adjust to them only gradually and then often with great difficulties. Social work's preoccupation with internal conflicts was therefore not out of place. The problem was that it was a young profession and built too much of its major method around the problems of this one specific era.

It took a long time for the profession to hear the warnings, which actually came early and never ceased. The capable and alert Mary Richmond saw potentials for social work beyond the too-narrow preoccupation with the individual. Influenced by Robert M. McIver's *Community* and Mary Parker Follett's *The New State*, and on the basis of her own observations, she stated in a paper in 1920:

Halfway between the minute analysis of the individual situation with which we are all familiar in casework and the kind of sixth sense of neighborhood standards, a background which is developed in a good social settlement, there is a field yet almost unexplored.

And further, she said, there is

a tendency in modern casework which I seem to have noted, and noted with great pleasure. It is one which is full of promise, I believe, for the future of social treatment. I refer to the new tendency to view our clients from the angle of what might be termed small group psychology.[19]

William Hodson, as executive secretary of the young professional

[19] Mary Richmond, "Some Next Steps in Social Treatment," *Proceedings*, National Conference of Social Work, 1920, pp. 254, 268.

organization, the American Association of Social Workers, sounded the warning note and put his finger on the conflict in social work in 1925 in his address "Is Social Work a Profession?"

Social work, then, is a form of service, which attempts, on the one hand, to help the individual or family group which is out of step to obtain more orderly rhythm in the march of existence and, on the other, to remove, so far as possible, the barriers, which obstruct others from achieving the best of which they are capable.

He spoke of casework and of dealing with individuals in groups.

Perhaps we can also avoid that too intense concentration upon the particular needs of the individual client which sometimes blinds the professions to a sense of responsibility to the community, by developing increasingly the ability to make our knowledge and experience count in prevention and reform.[20]

Jane Addams, who had been one of the first social workers to cross the line that separated the giver and the one given to, and who based her philosophy on strong religious and humanitarian ethical convictions, raised the question in an even sharper form in 1926. Speaking on the subject "How Much Social Work Can a Community Afford: From the Ethical Point of View?" she tried to combine the strong consideration of the individual which had developed in social work with a call for understanding social conditions. She also felt that social workers should have more courage in meeting the circumstances with which they were faced. She tried to combine recent scientific knowledge with ethical demands which she considered specific for social workers. Even if she did not completely succeed, she aimed at looking beyond old established attitudes. In her clear way she said, "We too are living on accumulated capital in spiritual and ethical affairs."

It was with some irony but also with a deep concern for the necessity of combining social responsibility with individual understanding when she called to her profession:

The leaders in this field of careful individual study are the psychiatric social workers. They are the newest and most popular group among

[20] William Hodson, "Is Social Work a Profession?" *Proceedings*, National Conference of Social Work, Denver, Colo., 1925 (Chicago: University of Chicago Press), pp. 631, 635.

us and perhaps we can ask a favor from them: that in time they go beyond this individual analysis and give us a little social psychiatric work.[21]

She referred here to something far more basic than a quarrel between different status groups in the social work profession. She was raising the question of the meaning of "adjustment." Was it only the individual client who had to do the "adjusting"? Here was the value conflict in the profession. Some members of the profession considered it their sole responsibility to help individuals to come to terms with their environment and with their inner conflict. This meant an acceptance of the status quo. On the other hand, there were social workers who considered "reform" the only goal of social work and resisted the concept of individual treatment. Jane Addams saw the urgent need to combine the two.

Eduard C. Lindeman entered the profession of social work at this stage in its development. It was a growing, self-conscious profession, preoccupied with methods and with intrapersonal conflicts, but not yet hardened into a mold. Recognizing its main tasks in the solving of intrapersonal and interpersonal problems and in the righting of social injustice, it had a broad streak of reform fervor and interest in community action, as well as interest in individual treatment. It was just beginning to train its own professional workers, drawing teachers from many different backgrounds.

Its values had been drawn not only from religion and from humanistic philosophies, but also from punitive thought systems and rigid moralistic approaches; its scientific base lay in economics, political science, sociology, psychology, and psychiatry. It had moved with these disciplines through different theories. When Lindeman entered the profession, its most developed part, casework, was strongly influenced by psychoanalytic theories. This affected the concept of "adjustment" and the hierarchy of values.

What did Lindeman bring to social work and how did the profession continue to develop in relation to its philosophical base?

---

[21] Jane Addams, "How Much Social Work Can a Community Afford: From the Ethical Point of View?" *Proceedings*, National Conference of Social Work, Cleveland, 1926, pp. 108–13.

CHAPTER 6

1920 TO 1930: COMMUNITY PROCESSES AND THE INDIVIDUAL'S ROLE IN THEM

Eduard Lindeman did not come to social work and social work education as a philosopher. Neither he nor his colleagues considered him such when he came to the New York School of Social Work. He was asked to teach at the young school because of his interest in community organization for welfare purposes and because of the contribution his book *The Community* had made to the thinking in this field. He was one of the first to establish principles of community organization and to actually observe and study the processes at work in communities.

In the first speech he gave at the National Conference of Social Work in 1920, he began to outline such principles. He called for a scientific approach to the problem of rural community organization. Psychology and sociology were the two scientific disciplines he considered. He deplored the fact that too much community organization was done by the trial-and-error method. He demanded as one of the first principles of good community organization an *investigation of facts* to give a better understanding of the dynamic forces of the community. A second principle was related to the need for coordination: "Community organization must take precedence over organization of the community by particularistic agencies or institutions." [1]

This paper was followed by *The Community*, the first book on community organization to appear, which expresses several prin-

[1] Lindeman, "Organization and Technique for Rural Recreation," *Proceedings*, National Conference of Social Work, 1920, p. 320.

ciples considered valid even today. Written during the period when Lindeman was influenced by his contact with the YMCA movement, it represented his sociological interest in rural community life as well as his persistent effort to make ideals live. In observing community life he was impressed by the conflict between specialists and laymen. The specialists were "apparently in conflict with some other current in modern life." [2] Lindeman recognized this other current as the demand of a democracy for the self-determination of citizens. The discussion of this conflict and an attempt to solve it formed the basis of *The Community*. The first step for specialists and citizens would be to agree on the goals of community life — on value-centered goals which could then be put into practice. It was Lindeman's conviction that agreement on general goals was comparatively easy: conflicts usually started with the discussion of *means*. To Lindeman the aim of all community life was "to bring about amicable relationships between men and groups of men." [3]

This general goal had to be spelled out and broken down into practical applications. In *The Community* Lindeman named nine such tangible community goals:

1. Order, or security of life and property through the medium of an efficient government.

2. Economic well-being, or security of income through an efficient system of productive industry.

3. Physical well-being, or health and sanitation through public health agencies.

4. Constructive use of leisure time, or recreation through organized and directed play.

5. Ethical standards, or a system of morality supported by the organized community.

6. Intellectual diffusion, or education through free and public institutions within the reach of all.

7. Free avenues of expression, or means by which all the elements of the community might freely express themselves; free newspapers and public forums.

8. Democratic forms of organization, or community-wide organization through which the entire community might express its thought and see that its will is done.

[2] Lindeman, *The Community*, p. viii.
[3] *Ibid.*, p. 1.

9. Spiritual motivation, or religious associations which might diffuse throughout all forms of community organization the religious or spiritual motive.[4]

He stressed the fact that these goals could never be completely reached and that there was always need for compromise. The community organizer should understand that people had different ideas about solutions to problems and that he could not expect that his ideas would always prevail. According to the principle of democracy he should accept expression of conflict. Neither the specialist nor the community group should completely dominate all decisions: "Thus it becomes evident that an extreme individualist theory carried to its logical conclusion ends in anarchy, and an extreme group theory ends in despotism."[5] We see here a method Lindeman used frequently: stating alternatives clearly and then moving away from an either-or solution.

The specialist must learn to work with all the forces in the community. Out of this principle grew Lindeman's constant emphasis on the importance of the *volunteer* and of *citizen participation* as builders of the basic force of community life. Specialist and citizen were dependent on each other for achieving a healthy community life, but they did not always realize this. *Interdependence* was a key word in Lindeman's concept of human relations.

Citizens become effective only by common group effort. No community organizer can force them into such groups; they will affiliate only with those groups they consider important to them. Lindeman called these groups "vital interest groups" and recommended study of them as essential for the community expert.[6] He pointed out that vital interest groups often develop into institutions — institutions demanding fierce loyalty which could lead to community strife:

Institutions are inevitable in organized society. And institutions in

[4] *Ibid.*, pp. 14–15.
[5] *Ibid.*, p. 64.
[6] In the opinion of this writer the concept of the vital interest group is an especially helpful one and one too little used and considered in modern community organization. It has been replaced by our concept of power structure which lends itself more readily to analysis. This latter concept leaves out of consideration whole segments of the population, knowledge of which is vital to the establishment of social services.

themselves are not harmful. They become social dangers when they proceed without a science and a philosophy. It is obvious to the most casual observer that our institutionalism lacks both scientific principles and philosophic basis. It has grown with but little conscious direction applied to it in relationship to larger social groups. Many of our social agencies have become vested interests; they lay claim to certain rights and privileges which they guard zealously. It is not an uncommon spectacle, in modern communities, to find social agencies involved in dissensions and quarrels, almost as deeply rooted and as prejudicial as the old religious animosities. This cannot, of course, go on with safety.[7]

This tendency of organizations to produce loyal members, and the tendency of this loyalty to interfere with the unified progress of the community, presented a dilemma. Lindeman saw its solution only in (1) learning more and more about the laws of voluntary aggregation and association among human beings — an understanding that would help one to be prepared for the development of such institutions and perhaps help to avoid exaggerated consequences; (2) increasing the interest of individuals and groups so that they learned to relate to an ever-increasing association: "The recognition of the fact that man's usefulness to mankind is enhanced by the increase of his social regard. . . . To narrow his interest is to restrict his social growth." [8] This warning was directed toward social agencies which sometimes endeavored to hold on to the loyalty of their members and make them feel guilty about their interest in other community activities. Lindeman asked the community organizer to recognize the emotional need of members to feel loyal to an agency and to accept its value, but he believed that the organizer should at the same time help community groups to maintain a rational view toward division of labor and planning.

By accepting the community member as an important and active part of social progress, the specialist had to depart from a concept of leadership based on doing *for* others. Leadership had to become an enabling process. "Each time the leader does something for the community that the community might have done for itself, he pre-

[7] Lindeman, *op. cit.*, p. 102.
[8] *Ibid.*, p. 103.

vents the community from developing its own resources." Lindeman stressed that in a democracy the group has a right to make its own mistakes. And with optimism he added, "Eventually this process leads to the proper utilization of specialized leadership." This optimism grew out of his basic conviction that "the fundamental and essential insights of life are within the reach of the so-called common man." [9]

These principles closely paralleled those in social casework which began a strong effort at this time to get away from the authoritarian and punitive heritage of the Poor Laws. The application of such principles to community organization was made first by Eduard Lindeman; this was the reason why his book met with such wide acclaim.

It was also in *The Community* that Lindeman presented the discussion method as a conflict-solving method in community organization:

It takes courage, the courage of firm convictions, to permit conflicts to appear in a public meeting. . . . But conflict is the only possible method by which ideas can be clarified in group action. . . . It may take more time, and it certainly requires infinitely more patience and faith in men to use the Democratic Process. . . . If Democracy cannot be applied to the problems of the small local community, how futile it is to speak of it as a national or an international ideal.[10]

This is a practical application of a recurring basic concept expressed by Lindeman: "facts infused with values." The specific value here was the democratic principle of free speech as it applies to the practical action of the community organizer in dealing with voluntary organizations. It was based on an increased understanding of the social process — an understanding which focused on both the individual and the group.

Lindeman established ten steps to be followed by the community organizer.

Step Number One. Consciousness of need; some person, either

[9] *Ibid.*, pp. 191, 195.
[10] *Ibid.*, p. 134.

within or without the community, expresses the need which is later represented by the definite project.

Step Number Two. Spreading the consciousness of need; a leader, within some institution or group within the community, convinces his or her group, or a portion of the group, of the reality of the need.

Step Number Three. Projection of consciousness of need; the group interest attempts to project the consciousness of need upon the leadership of the community; the consciousness of need becomes more general.

Step Number Four. Emotional impulse to meet the need quickly; some influential assistance is enlisted, in the attempt to arrive at a quick means of meeting the need.

Step Number Five. Presentation of other solutions; other means of meeting the need are presented.

Step Number Six. Conflict of solutions; various groups lend their support to one or the other of the various solutions presented.

Step Number Seven. Investigation; it appears to be increasingly customary to pause at this point, and to investigate the project with expert assistance. (This step, however, is usually omitted and the following one takes its place.)

Step Number Eight. Open discussion of issue; a public mass meeting or gathering of some sort is held, at which the project is presented, and the groups with most influence attempt to secure adoption of their plans.

Step Number Nine. Integration of solutions; the various solutions presented are tested, with an effort to retain something out of each, in the practicable solution which is now emerging.

Step Number Ten. Compromise on basis of tentative progress; certain groups relinquish certain elements of their plans in order to save themselves from complete defeat, and the solution which results is a compromise with certain reservations. The means selected for meeting the need are not satisfactory to all groups, but are regarded as tentatively progressive.[11]

Recent social work literature on community organization has not moved far from the method outlined by Lindeman. It is one of the errors of the profession that it seldom builds on work done earlier. In the article on community organization in the *Social Work Year-book of 1954* there is no reference to this important book. That article dates the community organization movement as beginning

[11] *Ibid.*, pp. 123–24.

in 1938 when it set up a section at the National Conference of Social Work. The historical view would help social work to move faster and to enrich its theory by using the thinking of many.

The Community contains the elements of Lindeman's basic approach to human problems: (1) the constant awareness of the value component in facts and (2) an *ever-searching* and questioning attitude, so well expressed by Gotthold Ephraim Lessing, the eighteenth-century German philosopher, in his *Anti-Götze*: "If God should hold enclosed in his right hand all truth, and in his left hand only the ever-active searching after truth, although with the condition that I must always and forever err, I would with humility turn to his left hand and say, 'Father, give me this: Ultimate truth is for Thee alone.'"

The practical approach was Lindeman's strength. He did not establish a new philosophical system. Rather, his contribution lay in the application of philosophical thought to everyday questions and in his constant endeavor to bring to social work the knowledge gained from the humanities. His dislike of the use of a dogmatic system was often expressed when he discussed such attempts made by others — Hegel or Marx, for instance. It was most clearly expressed in the introduction to Part II of *Dynamic Social Research*. Under the heading "Evolving Social Philosophy," we find:

Much of the difficulty in scientific reasoning is to be attributed to the fact that thinkers, especially original thinkers, are likely to regard their categories as absolutes and ultimates. Once they have hit upon a term or phrase which is pregnant with meaning they somehow or other allow their emotions to become attached to the word; they become protagonists for verbal symbols. Words are, of course, nothing but symbols, and concepts are merely tools to be used in reasoning and in communicating meanings to others. The procedure for deriving suitable categories for any given scientific context belongs primarily to philosophy. A "good" category is one which stands meaningfully by itself and at the same time bears an "organic" relation to the whole, that is, the whole of any given set of concepts belonging to a selected area of discourse. . . .[12]

[12] John J. Hader and Eduard C. Lindeman, *Dynamic Social Research* (New York: Harcourt, 1933), pp. 38, 211, 213.

(It was significant that his criticism of Tolstoy in *The Community* was that he experimented with Christianity by running away from the problems of the modern community, a method Lindeman rejected.)

An addendum to *The Community* is presented "as merely a statement of the positive portions of my present faith. No finality is attached to any section." The basic tenets of this faith were

1. The teachings of Jesus — if really applied — could help solve the world's social, economic and political problems.

2. Science and Religion belong together. The one searches for what is, the other for what should be.

3. The concept of Evolution means constant change. The human being can and must control this movement, if he wants to achieve progress. If he does not make this effort, there will be retrogression.

4. The insights in life are in the reach of every man. He must be allowed to think freely, even if there is disagreement. Yet nobody can stand alone. The Human family is destined to rise or fall as a unit.

5. Democracy is a way of life, which allows the individual to come to greatest fulfillment while at the same time working toward the common good.

This was the framework of values Lindeman presented in the early years, before his close association with the group around the Inquiry and with John Dewey. The religious component was stronger at this time than it was in his middle years, but he later returned to it with some modification. He constantly tried to combine religious convictions and scientific thought. In 1911, in one of his earliest writings, he said that he wanted "religion without prejudice and faith in science." [13] His emphasis on the possibility of uniting religion and science was so strong that it seems as if he had to battle his own fundamentalist background and to prove to himself that there was no contradiction between religious and scientific thought. At this time his concept of religion was extremely individualistic and he considered it purely subjective.[14] Slowly this concept changed.

In a 1924 speech on "The Religion of a Scientist" he referred to

[13] Lindeman, *College Characters, Essays and Verse*, p. 68.
[14] See "The Religion of a Scientist" (an outline), *New Haven Forum*, March 16, 1924.

William James's *Varieties of Religious Experience*, pointing out that religion and science could go together because the ultimate authority for both was experience — provided that the religion was not dogmatic. He saw the Christian way of life as the application of principles to specific problems and the evolving of new principles out of those problems. He tried to clarify his distinction between science and religion by saying that action based on facts was science, whereas action based on faith was religion.

Permeating Lindeman's writings is his struggle with the question of ethics and religion and their subjectivity. In a speech given in Denmark in 1924 he said that the religious quest is the central search of people's lives.[15] Shortly before his death, on January 28, 1953, in his letter to Laura Pratt thanking her for helping with the plan for the establishment of the Lindeman Chair, he suggested to his unknown successor that "he dedicate himself to the task of bringing social work into a realistic alignment with religion and ethics." During this span of approximately thirty years he continued to develop his idea of ethics and religion.

He was never close to organized religion. His demand for ethical conduct was never completely fulfilled by the churches he knew, as excerpts from a pamphlet he wrote in 1929 show. The pamphlet, *The Church in the Changing Community*, gave a clear picture of what he expected from organized religion. He started out by describing the characteristics of urbanism: impersonal relationships between people, disintegration of neighborhood life, powerful interest groups, rapid movement of individuals in space, and much overstimulation. He criticized the church for not having adapted to this changing environment. By this time, he had given up the highly individualistic religion he had held to earlier in his life, and specifically disagreed with this concept. Religion should be part of everyday conduct and, therefore, a social force. The church's purpose should be to give "tone and color to the community's social climate, to vitalize its resources." It should provide fellowship among human beings. It should put its greatest emphasis on the *participating* member of the church community. He defined this kind of member-

---

[15] "The Philosopher's Stone," unpublished MS.

ship as "that body of persons which is at any given moment acting in relation to the group. . . . Members would be immediately recognized as the visible, moving, functioning participators." This was his expression of the importance of group life and group participation and his rejection of authority of the church in a community. He saw as the function of the church "training for value-determination — the means of sensitizing people to an atmosphere of pervading values." The method used to help people to understand the ends for which the church stood should be the small group process.[16]

The recurring theme was that faith should not be separated from action. Religion meant living ethics, and ethics should permeate all of one's life. In 1923 he said to an audience of social workers:

If ethics are to function in the family but not in the chamber of commerce, in the church, but not in the board of directors, in the Rotary Club, but not in the factory — then we may as well have no ethics, for the places where we talk about ethics are relatively unimportant while the places where we act significantly shape our lives and other lives and determine whether we are building a miserable or a joyful world.[17]

What was Lindeman's relationship in these years to the concepts of *individual* and *society* which are vital to the building of a theoretical system?

In the 1920s we find three major theories of psychology in the United States of America:

1. Psychology as an inquiry into the conscious mind of man was represented by William James in the United States and Wilhelm Max Wundt in Germany. They based many of their observations on experiment and were closely related to the physical school of thought which accepted the existence of inborn instincts.

2. John B. Watson's behaviorism investigated only overt expressions and rejected the concept of consciousness as too religious. To Watson the idea of consciousness was too close to the idea of the

[16] Lindeman, *The Church in the Changing Community* (New York: The Community Church, 1929), pp. 12, 16, 21.

[17] Lindeman, "Industrial Technique and Social Assets," *Proceedings*, National Conference of Social Work, 1923, pp. 130–36.

human being's having a soul to be acceptable. He believed that men reacted only because of conditioned reflexes. "No one has ever touched a soul"; therefore it could not exist. To Watson and his school introspection could not be a tool of psychology because it dealt with intangibles and was unscientific. Watson, in his effort to make psychology a natural science, forced psychologists to do more exact research. At the same time, he could not avoid the value judgments inherent in all psychological endeavor; but he forgot to make the distinction between what is and what should be. His claims were astonishingly great: "Behavioristic efforts, experimental in type, which will tell us whether it is advisable from the standpoint of present or future adjustments of the individual to have one wife or several: to have capital punishment or punishment of any kind . . ." He could not avoid the temptation of many twentieth-century psychologists and sociologists to assume that if the world followed his rules it would be saved. "Behaviorism does lay a foundation for saner living. . . . For the universe will change if you bring up your children, not in the freedom of the libertine but in behavioristic freedom. . . . until the world finally becomes a place fit for human habitation." [18]

3. The psychological system which influenced social work most strongly was the one based on Freud's experience with psychoanalysis. Freud, a physician, was schooled in the biological sciences and therefore tended to use clinical experience instead of speculative theories. Only in his later years did he, too, fail to distinguish clearly between what *is* and what *should be*. He became almost mystical in his application of psychoanalytic thinking.[19] Freud's psychology was more closely related to William James's than to Watson's. He agreed with James that the human being has inborn instincts and like James he inquired into the nature of man by introspection. Unlike James's school, however, he let the patient speak for himself, and he stressed the significance of unconscious motivation. It is important to

[18] John B. Watson, *Behaviorism* (New York: Norton, 1924–25), pp. 4, 7, 248.

[19] Sigmund Freud, *Moses and Monotheism*, Katherine Jones, tr. (New York: Knopf, 1939).

realize that his theory had different meanings in the contexts of the different cultures into which it was introduced. In Central Europe it meant a revolution and a liberation of the individual from the authoritarian influence of the father in the family and the monarch in the state. It was therefore welcomed by the young revolutionary forces, especially in Germany and Austria. In the United States, on the other hand, it intensified an already existing individualistic attitude and found its way mainly into the upper middle class which resisted any encroachment on individual rights. Freud laid great emphasis on the unity of mind and body and helped psychology to move away from a dualism which was perpetuated by Watson and James.

Through his voluminous reading Lindeman had been exposed to these three schools of psychology. It was typical of his way of dealing with theories that from the beginning he looked for integration. In the *New Republic* in 1924 he said:

The emerging philosophy of our time will not be concerned over the mind-body problem. Its approach to human nature will be the approach to a psycho-physical entity in which any separation of mind from body will be regarded as sheer mysticism. Man will be observed as a behaving organism in a continuing process of adjustment to his physical and social environment. The adjusting process will be viewed not as the organism acting upon the environment, or vice versa, but rather as a process of interaction in which all factors of the adjusting process undergo modification.[20]

It was inconceivable to Lindeman that he could become a dogmatic adherent of one school of thought. His concept of the individual human being was formed out of his acquaintance with psychiatry, social psychology, philosophy, and other disciplines. He had read William James intensively and felt close to him in his philosophical thinking, but he did not adopt his psychology. Though he never

[20] Lindeman, "Emerging American Philosophy," *New Republic*, November 19, 1924, Vol. XXXX, pp. 290–91. It is amazing how much this thought anticipates present-day thinking in psychology and psychiatry (compare the recent writings of Sandor Rado and Nathan Ackerman). Yet to make our present-day generation even more humble I quote from Leibnitz: "Since the world is a plenum all things are connected together and everybody acts upon every other, more or less, according to their distance, and is affected by their reaction . . ." (Leibnitz, *Principles of Nature and Grace*, Paragraph 3).

seemed to feel very comfortable with Freudian theory, he used psychoanalytic concepts quite early in his writings. In *The Community* in 1921 he described the nature of man as dynamic and he spoke of some of the inborn instincts, one of which is to survive. He said in a speech in 1922 that "No one can be a good altruist unless he is also a good egoist." [21] This is an expression of Freudian thinking which underlines the fact that the human being needs to receive love before he can give love.

The famous speech at the Recreation Congress in 1922 which inspired Walter Pettit to want the young Lindeman to become a member of the faculty of the School of Social Work set forth Lindeman's eclectic view of the nature of man. He spoke of the "new psychology" but obviously did not mean Watson's, of which this expression was also used. Lindeman's understanding of the human being as set forth in this speech was based on four concepts.

1. The human being is a whole; it is an entity of body and soul, of thought and feeling.

2. "We are no longer slaves to our instincts." This expresses a movement away from James's inherited-instinct theory.

3. People can act rationally: "Within the new psychology is the hope for a new rational center of optimism."

4. An unconscious mind exists which is not necessarily a determining factor for action but must be considered as existing. "There is considerable significance in the discoveries of psychoanalysis . . ." [22] To Lindeman no contradiction existed between the acceptance of the existence of an unconscious and the knowledge that people can and should act rationally. Freud himself had never doubted this, but some of his followers had put far too much stress on the irrational.

Lindeman's interest in the individual centered mainly on the individual's relationship to others and his contribution to society. Lindeman's was not a clinical interest; as one of his colleagues, Gordon Hamilton, pointed out: he was not "problem centered." His

[21] Lindeman, "The Place of the Local Community in Organized Society," *Proceedings*, National Conference of Social Work, 1922, pp. 67–77.
[22] Lindeman, "Recreation and the New Psychology," *The Playground*, Vol. XVII, No. 4, July 1923, pp. 212, 246, 447.

interest was in the *strength* of people. He regarded the individual as a whole with no division between mind and body. The human being must be understood as interacting with his environment and with others, as a rational being with the capacity to choose between conflicting values, and influenced by conscious as well as unconscious drives. He becomes a healthy and integrated person when he receives recognition from others and gives rights to others, when he assumes responsibilities and honors other human beings and their cultural achievement.

Similarly, his concept of society was not related to one particular school of sociology. He had been exposed to the Middlewestern (especially Chicago) school of sociologists and their growing interest in understanding subcultures. He had been impressed by W. I. Thomas's and Florian Znaniecki's *Polish Peasant* and its intensive investigation of segments of the community.[23] He had read Karl Marx and Adam Smith and — influenced by Lester Ward — he objected to the deterministic as well as to the laissez-faire concept of society.[24]

Like psychology, sociology was a child of the twentieth century. It, too, had originally been part of philosophy. Because of their interest in ethics, all philosophers had to investigate society. Yet this inquiry, like that of philosophers into psychology, was more speculative than a strict observation of actual processes: "The *political* factor under the dominance of a purely ethical interest, the interest in the good life . . . was given priority over the social factor." [25]

Twentieth-century sociology imposed upon itself the rigid discipline of observation. Though it succeeded far better than psychology in getting away from speculative theories, it, too, since it dealt with human relations, could not escape the influence of values. Right up to the present there is controversy between sociologists who think that they can teach "pure facts" removed from any value system and

[23] William Isaac Thomas and Florian Znaniecki, *The Polish Peasant in Europe and America* (New York: Knopf, 1927).

[24] See Notebook 1944 and Lindeman's review of Laski's *The American Democracy*.

[25] Robert M. MacIver, "Sociology" in the *Encyclopedia of the Social Sciences*, Vol. XIV (New York: Macmillan, 1934), p. 233.

sociologists who consider this impossible. Robert MacIver says: "It is not here assumed that the interest of the ethical thinker and that of the social scientist are irreconcilable." [26]

Since MacIver belonged to the same group of the Inquiry as Lindeman, it can be assumed that they influenced each other. They did not belong to Pareto's school of objective social science, which ran parallel to Watson's psychology. Lindeman's interest was in understanding society so that it could be influenced. He distinguished between culture and civilization, assigning to culture the role of determining the ends and goals of human life and to civilization the means to achieve them. To him, cultural lag meant the discrepancy between the two. Since human beings are capable of changing their institutions, they should strive to diminish this lag. This could best be done through small groups which are the important cells out of which society was formed.

The primary group in society is the family, which gives the individual stability and the feeling of intimate social unity. As an institution the family had gone through different stages and to Lindeman it appeared "that we are now at work building the democratic family." [27] The fact that society was working to establish maternity insurance, prevent exploitation of women in industry, teach constructive use of leisure time, protect child labor and equal property, and assure political and social rights for all men and women were to him signs of the change toward a more democratic family.

Secondary groups are those the individual chooses or those which have become established institutions of society. Lindeman's special interest was in the first kind — the chosen groups which in *The Community* he called the "vital interest groups," and in the smaller local unit, the community. Both *The Community* and *Social Discovery* were investigations into the rural community. In *Social Discovery*, written in 1924, he made a special point of the importance of describing social conduct as clearly as possible to gain understanding. As Herbert Croly said in the Introduction, "The primary function of the social discoverer is to understand. In relation to

[26] *Ibid.*, p. 233.
[27] Lindeman, *The Community*, p. 20.

action it must always be expressed in alternatives rather than in absolute objectives . . . he is never seeking or expecting a consummation. He is always seeking additional discovery." [28]

To Lindeman social science was an audit of social activities by a participant observer. He accepted the concepts of class structure, ethnic groupings, and power struggle, but did not use these in a universal sense. It was impossible for him to explain society in the framework of one concept alone. He neither adhered to the theory of economic determinism nor denied the importance of economic power. He did not accept the hypothesis that all community relations are based on power structures nor did he deny the existence and importance of such structures. He did not accept the theory of the "great men" nor did he deny the role that leaders play in the shaping of society. His concept of society was pluralistic. To the forces mentioned he added the importance of ideas and ideals in shaping society.[29]

Social Discovery was written after Lindeman's close contact with a group of outstanding pragmatists. In it he named as his chief sources William James, Mary Parker Follett, Mrs. Alfred Dwight Sheffield, and Herbert Croly. His philosophy had moved away from the strongly religious motivation of *The Community*. Characteristic of Lindeman's philosophy at this period is a page at the end of *Social Discovery* headed "Social Ethics and Social Philosophy."

The impact of the foregoing chapters considered as a unit is unmistakably critical, realistic, and perhaps without that element of inspiring impulse for which readers ordinarily and justifiably turn to social sciences. The exclusion was inevitable. Truth is whatever is found to be general "within a clearly defined part of existence"; this essay purports to aid in the search for truth by directing thought and investigation toward a method which may help to define a highly important part of existence. The good life is irretrievably bound up with and conditioned by the modern complex of group organizations in which we live and have our being; it cannot be released until this complex is scientifically and intellectually unravelled. Whatever is

---

[28] Lindeman, *Social Discovery* (New York: Republic Publishing Co., 1924, 1936), p. xviii.
[29] See *The Community*, p. 26, *Social Discovery*, p. 360, *Dynamic Social Research*, p. 18, and various notebooks.

potentially beautiful in the relations between human beings lies partially dormant because these relations remain as mystifying and falsifying barriers. Whatever capacities for freedom lie within the scope of human nature now lie inert, nay, are atrophied by increasing and blind obeisance to collectivism considered as an end. How may life generate expressions of the true, the good and the beautiful? There is no answer in wishing, believing, exhorting. There is no answer save one: the truth is that which is understood and the good is that which has been tested in the light of understanding.[30]

This was an expression of orthodox pragmatism. No general values could be accepted; the good could only be understood in light of experience. The disillusionment of the war and postwar periods induced Lindeman to turn away from high-sounding phrases, but his answers were mainly investigation into "what is." To a man who had always fought for causes and who had very definite ideas about social justice, this must have been quite an unsatisfactory period. The pragmatic view helped him and remained with him all his life as a tool to test reality in terms of the applicability of ethical values. But the strict interpretation of the good in terms only of what was workable soon changed to become the demand to make the good workable. In a 1946 notebook he remarked that he must deal with faith and doubt "as inseparable links in the chain of reasoning." In this way he had come to terms with the conflict between critical appraisal and basic belief. Science and religion no longer seemed incompatible.

Because of his practical interest in the study of society, he wrote and thought more about the contemporary American scene than about general theories of society. He did not agree with Harold J. Laski's *The American Democracy*, but he accepted much of Laski's interpretation of America's tradition: its belief in progress; its dynamic concept of civilization; its expansionism; its pioneering; its individual empiricism, pragmatism, and universal passion for physical property; its middle-class values and enlightened self-interest; its activism and political democracy; its low-grade civil service; its belief in education; and its class mobility. He saw its tradition as nonmilitary and religious, as embodying a belief in

[30] Lindeman, *Social Discovery*, p. 364.

government by law not by men — expressed in the supremacy of the judiciary — and he realized its tendency toward optimism and its lack of feudal tradition.

What he missed on the United States scene, especially in the years before 1934, was a candid expression of an American culture. Music, drama, and play had not yet become an expression of a country which had grown out of many nations. This expression was an ideal toward which he worked and he considered the wise use of leisure time an important tool in achieving the goal.

In Lindeman's speech, "Recreation and the New Psychology," he expressed a beginning philosophy of social work with special emphasis on recreation: Society had moved into the century when the automatic machine had become an essential part of life. It had become important for the human mind to control the machine consciously and effectively. Lindeman disagreed with Marxist determinism: "The only kind of determinism I believe in is a determinism which results from the cooperative thinking of human minds." He thought it important that social workers should develop a philosophy of life related to this machine-age development, and then out of a philosophy technique would grow. The purposive and constructive use of leisure time, he earnestly believed, was one way of controlling the machine age.

To Lindeman play and recreation fulfilled two demands: (1) they provided "progress . . . which creates better human relations through mental release" and (2) they could give to people opportunities for participating — not only getting people together — but participating in some significant activity. Recreation would provide opportunity for intelligent functioning within the highly mechanized industrial process. It could fulfill the purpose of making people think and it could be the means by which they learn "not to fear a new idea." It also could provide the human being with a balance not afforded in his daily work. It could help toward better citizenship as well as toward better mental health. Lindeman's concepts of society, of the role of recreation at this time in history, and of the role social work played in community organization led him into further investigation of the relationship between the citizen and the professional worker.[31]

In several papers following *The Community*, Lindeman stressed the necessity for cooperation between expert and citizen:

The most significant phenomenon relating to this subject is to be found, not in the minds of social workers, but in the minds of laymen, of citizens. . . . After all, human relations are adjusted in human ways. If it is assumed that only the trained social worker has any part to play in social adjustment will not this assumption separate the social worker from the normal social process?[32]

His emphasis on the importance of the volunteer and the layman was related to his basic respect for the dignity of those who wanted to help themselves. He took the principle of the dignity of men seriously and repeated that it was important to avoid professional conceit. In 1921 when he was still close to rural life he asserted that the Grange was the social movement which had to be respected by those who wanted to help the farmers in other areas of community organization. He described how the farm families looked with suspicion upon social agencies which might consider them an "object of reform." In rural areas he saw evidence of progress in the social work that was being started under government auspices; such sponsorship made receiving help not charity but a citizen's right. He also welcomed the use of trained personnel who would understand the philosophy of self-help.[33]

He insisted that the trained community organizer and social worker should make every effort to understand the specific needs of his clientele. He should not use the same methods in work with farmers that he used in the city. There were serious problems in rural areas: upset family relationships, disease, and lack of educational facilities and social life. Social workers were needed, yet they should be grounded in details of farm life and its resulting psychology.

Lindeman's future colleague, Philip Klein, who was at that time

[31] Lindeman, "Recreation and the New Psychology," *The Playground*, Vol. XVII, No. 4, July 1923, pp. 211, 213, 2.

[32] Lindeman, "The Place of the Local Community in Organized Society," *Proceedings*, National Conference of Social Work, 1922, pp. 67–77.

[33] Lindeman, "Organization of Rural Social Causes," *Proceedings*, National Conference of Social Work, 1921, pp. 12–22.

the director of the Rural Service of the Southern Division of the American Red Cross in Atlanta, Georgia, contradicted him sharply in regard to his emphasis on specifics. He insisted that rural problems were not different from urban ones. He agreed that there were not enough educational opportunities, but contended that this was no different from the situation in the cities. Klein maintained that "to us as social workers there falls the comparatively humble lot of bringing to the country and adapting to rural conditions the type of social work we have been doing in the cities and to bring it to the same degree of efficiency that we have attained in the cities." [34] Both men showed equal concern with their task. The controversy arose from their diverging evaluation of facts.

We find a similar difference of opinion today concerning social work in other countries. Some social workers think that American methods of social work can be directly transferred to other countries, while others believe considerable change is necessary when the methods are used in a different culture. The solution of this controversy will come only through the conscious testing of experience.

An article written in 1923 showed Lindeman's growing interest in the wide function he delegated to social work. He insisted that social workers should think of more than simply correcting maladjustments. While the doctor, the teacher, and the preacher could be highly specialized and narrow their functions, the social worker had to

perforce extend his base of operations to include the whole of life. He deals with the total personality. The fundamental basis of his technique involves a conscious attempt to promote progress, and progress is measurable only in terms of status. Status includes the various modes according to which the individual expresses his personality on the economic, social, intellectual and moral levels. [35]

He saw the social worker as a liaison between privileged and underprivileged people; as a helper in human relations and in working with community forces; as the equalizer of opportunities; as the

[34] Philip Klein, "Discussion of Dr. Lindeman's Paper," *Proceedings*, National Conference of Social Work, 1921, p. 410.
[35] Lindeman, "The Social Worker and His Community," *Survey Graphic*, Vol. LII, April 15, 1924, pp. 83–85.

rescuer of the maladjusted, educator in values, and idealizer of life. The latter was particularly characteristic of Lindeman, who insisted that part of social work's task was the improvement of culture.

In another article in *Survey Graphic* he called Jane Addams the symbol of statesmanship who had influenced community forces, but not as a manipulator — not for personal ends. She had shown that social work must not serve negative ends only, but "must adopt a program and a technique which deals with the entire scope of human adjustments. For this task, statesmanship of high order is needed. Mere technicians will not suffice." [36]

After Lindeman joined the faculty of the New York School of Social Work his interest in social work grew, as is evident from the content of a 1926 article in the *New Republic*, "From Social Work to Social Science." It was an intensive analysis of the 53rd Annual Meeting of the National Conference of Social Work in Cleveland. This article is unsigned, but it must have been written by Lindeman — because this was the time when the coverage of such conferences was his assignment, because it is written in his style, and because many thoughts in it coincide with material in his notebook. This article is especially significant as an expression of Lindeman's thinking about social work in the twenties. It shows his sharp criticism of the profession when it did not come up to its promises and it also indicates his increasing identification with the profession.

In it, he called the convention one of "craftsmen, an exchange of technical experience among those whose business it is to exemplify the beneficent and humane spirit of the American people." He commented on the increased specialization and diversification of social work and on its importance to national life. For these reasons, he thought it necessary to investigate the motives, the disciplines, and the results of this growing profession. He criticized some of the "subtle hypocrisies" which crept into charity. Too often, he said, there were selfish motives behind the giving, and it was done more to glorify the giver than to help the one in need. "And when virtuous giving is administered by committees and employed specialists self-

[36] Lindeman, "The Social Worker as Statesman," *Survey Graphic*, Vol. LII, May 15, 1924, pp. 222–24.

deception spreads. This is not to say that we are able to escape self-deceit — any of us — but merely that vocational justification of an essentially selfish act in terms of compensating altruism is one of the great dangers which confronts every person who sets forth to do good to his fellow man." Lindeman did not say that all social workers were guilty of this self-deceit but he called sternly for self-examination. If this self-examination was not undertaken, then the client would suffer. "Politics, religion and charity — sinners all against the spirit of science, against freedom, and against a certain kind of personal integrity: and perhaps charity is still the greatest of these three disciplines of life — greatest in guilt and in promise. . . ." The guilt would be increased if social work continued to engage only in ameliorative activities. But he also disagreed with those critics who wanted only to change society and who forgot the individual. He saw hope in the "forward rank of social workers," creators of "a new technique, a new philosophy, and a new spirit, which, if it succeeds in winning the day will transform old-style philanthropy into a genuine social therapeutics."

The new social work, he emphasized, understood that the total process of adjustment must include help for the individual *and* change of social organizations.

Adjustment consequently is a dual process: the forms of social organization need to be adjusted in such manner as to produce cohesion among the constituent units, and the individuals need to be adjusted to the social forms without sacrificing their essential freedom. Professional social workers of the past have been over-eager to bring pressure to bear upon individuals out of adjustment, but they have not been equally zealous critics of social institutions. Younger social workers — younger, that is, in method — now see that they cannot become instruments of one-sided adjustment without at the same time becoming conservative props for all existing forms of social control; they begin to realize that professional self-respect demands that they too, labor on the side of freedom. The social diagnostician who places all of the blame for maladjustment upon the individual and none upon the social order must in the end become servile to those whose interests are vested in that order. He must, in short, become a tool of the power-groups. This is what the young workers are beginning to see with considerable clarity. They will not be contented to enter a profession which aims to minister to the unadjusted, dependent, delinquent and defective individuals of society without being at the same time free to inquire into the ways by which such a society is manipulated, the ways by which the accepted social process itself becomes one of the causes of maladjustment.

Social therapeutics means, not doing good to people, but helping them to find out how to do good by themselves. . . .

Lindeman saw the impetus that mental hygiene had given to social work. He looked upon it more dispassionately than did those among the social workers who viewed psychoanalysis as the new panacea for mankind. He saw mental hygiene in the framework of American culture. One can almost see him smile as he described American culture's emphasis on individualistic approach and told how mental hygiene concepts fitted this approach. "Show an American citizen with means and a disposition to be generous to an individual in distress and he will invariably be moved to aid. Show this same citizen a group and he will find the greatest difficulty in visualizing distress."

Yet while he recognized the importance of the individualistic approach, he also wanted to make sure that social workers saw wider issues. In the *New Republic* article is this almost-prophetic paragraph:

Here then is a new force in social work and for the most part a wholesome one. We shall, of course, carry the psychiatric emphasis too far — if indeed we have not already done so. Social workers equipped with psychiatric technique will develop blind spots. They will, like all devotees of fashions, upset the balance, throw the entire line of advance out of proportion, and in their apostolic excitement they will band themselves into cults. They will, that is, become separatists and in so far as they detach themselves from other specialists will become dogmatic partisans. Nothing, of course, is worse for science, but now that the dangers are evident the evil effects may be minimized by good-natured foresight.

It is clear today that overemphasis on psychiatry in social work was not avoided. There were always those, however, who warned against it and those who used it wisely — as discussed earlier with reference to a paper by Jane Addams (see pp. 100–101).[37]

Lindeman was in tune with the part of the social work profession which saw dangers in too much emphasis on technique. Outstanding examples of such thinking were Miriam Van Waters' papers at the 1929 and 1930 National Conferences of Social Work, the second given as the presidential address. Portions of them are given here for purposes of comparing Lindeman's approach with those of other prominent social workers of his time.

In the 1929 paper Miriam Van Waters said, "At present we note the immaturity of the social worker's ethics. His morality is a portrait of himself with his background. His values are fixed less by personal conviction than by prevailing tendencies of scientific thought and social approval."[38] Her work in correctional institutions had made her familiar with a variety of cultural backgrounds and she had been confronted with a corresponding variety of value systems. For this reason she was particularly conscious of the necessity for a social worker to re-examine his accepted values in the light of his present knowledge. She wanted social workers to be courageous in questioning old values, and cautioned them against acting uncritically on the basis of values inherent in their own early environments.

When she became president of the National Conference in 1930 she chose as the topic for her presidential address "Philosophical Trends in Modern Social Work." Her basic approach to social work was that it was "an attitude and a system of ideas." Her philosophical understanding of social work was that it considered the human scene as a *whole*, "for social work is international in scope and interracial. Its methodology is useful in solving the human problems of the happy and adequate, as well as the handicapped and unhappy." This statement about the wholeness of the profession and its universal character sounded a new note, with far-reaching implications for the profession. It moved the profession away from a sharp separation between the "adequate" and the "inadequate" in society, recog-

---

[37] "From Social Work to Social Science," *New Republic*, June 2, 1926.

[38] Miriam Van Waters, "New Morality and Social Workers," *Proceedings*, National Conference of Social Work, San Francisco, 1929, p. 79.

nizing that while people needed help at times, this did not make them "inadequate people." With the acceptance of this concept the social worker was no longer an all-powerful being, but a professional helper to those who needed him at a particular time.

Miriam Van Waters used the historical method to develop this philosophy. She described social work's beginnings in the almshouses, the jails — expressions of the belief that inadequacy is an inherited quality; through a period of preoccupation with problems of administration — the era of placing children in the country and of great emphasis on investigation and registration; through the years of interest in mental development — particularly as it is related to inadequacy; to the radical departure early in this century away from all these preoccupations and toward an emphasis on the social environment — the era of social legislation, preventive work, and neighborhood work: "A sense of social relationships was dawning."

She considered the decade from 1914 to 1924 a period of self-consciousness and self-criticism, with their attendant advantages and disadvantages. This was the time of Mary Richmond's great formulation of social casework, the learning of record-keeping, and evaluation of practice. It was the time of the application of the concepts of mental hygiene to the understanding of the individual human being.

Like Jane Addams, she criticized the narrow concept of "adjustment" which had developed in some parts of social work.

Social workers at conferences peered anxiously into the faces of their comrades with the unspoken question: Have you been psychoanalyzed? Indeed, there was no need to ask. The freshly analyzed social worker is immediately discernible. His speech is both cryptic and dogmatic. His curiosity about the way of life of his friends is second only to his intense preoccupation with his new self.

This biting indictment apparently was not directed against a tendency among social workers to gain more self-awareness. She was concerned that social workers should become social *thinkers* who could look beyond themselves and the individual problems of their clients and become sensitive to standards of life, "the vision of life abundant."

COMMUNITY PROCESSES AND THE INDIVIDUAL'S ROLE   127

In her philosophical discussion she stressed the need for seeing a person's problems as a whole and understanding the individual as such, but also for seeing him in the context of societal forces. While she was condemning the exaggerated preoccupation with intrapersonal problems she also rejected the "social reformer who adopts a program of hatred." She believed that the social worker should see "the suffering individual as an integral part of the whole, not as a burden but as a challenge." The social worker's attitude toward the human being should be closest to the thinking of Spinoza, who aimed "neither to revile nor to deride but to understand human conduct." [39]

In his early contact with social work Lindeman brought to the profession his concern with social policy and its translation into community action. He was almost completely removed from that part of the profession which developed the casework method. He was interested in and studied some of the psychological theories underlying it, but did not contribute to its working through of the method.

Through his close association with the group around John Dewey and the Inquiry he brought to social work the emphasis on an inquiring mind and the necessity for a more flexible attitude — an attitude allowing for rethinking of given theories.

Concepts which he contributed and stressed during this first period were (1) the value of constant inquiry and change; (2) the necessity and acceptance of conflict as a dynamic force; (3) the acceptance of the fact of unconscious motivation combined with the capacity of the human being to act rationally; (4) the pluralistic concept of society; (5) social work as a profession which deals with the whole of life and is therefore concerned with the individual in his environment, in groups, in adjustment of the deprived person as well as the adjustment of society to individual needs; (6) social work as a partnership between the professional worker and the citizen.

[39] Miriam Van Waters, "Philosophical Trends in Modern Social Work," *Proceedings*, National Conference of Social Work, Boston, 1930, pp. 3–19.

CHAPTER 7

1930 TO 1940: THE DEVELOPMENT OF SOCIAL GROUP WORK, SOCIAL RESEARCH, AND WELFARE PLANNING

THE reform movement had lost much of its impetus by 1930. Social work was trying to find its way from an idealistic general concern about human conditions to a combination of this concern with scientific inquiry and teachable methods. The methods of social group work and community organization began to develop. The settlement movement had relied on the conscience of the layman, but had not found a Mary Richmond to clearly define and develop its own teachable method. In the words of Frank Bruno: "When finally the technique of social group work was defined, neither the term nor its definition came from the settlement field, although the settlement has from the start operated with groups more realistically and experimentally than any existing institution." [1]

The strongest new impulse came from another field: progressive education. In 1920 a small group of educators, social workers, and psychologists in New York began to be interested in the relation of free group discussion and group action to democracy. It investigated social processes. In 1923 the first course in group work in a school of social work was started at Western Reserve University.[2]

The method of *social group work* was developed in close relation to community organization. Lindeman was an active participant in

[1] Frank J. Bruno, *Trends in Social Work* (New York: Columbia University Press, 1948), p. 119.

[2] There is no written history of the development of the group work method but there is a doctoral dissertation on the subject being prepared by Charles Levy at the New York School of Social Work.

this effort. He saw in group work a tool for free discussion, for helping citizens to establish more effective committee work, and for helping the growth of indigenous leadership. He never thought of group work as related only to leisure-time agencies, though these made up an important part of the social work picture. Rather he considered the group work method important for community action, adult education, and mental hygiene. A notebook kept later in his life (October 1951–March 1953) gives this concise description: "Group work is a mental hygiene experience — a venture in sanity. Small groups, conscious discipline in human relations, nuclear democracy, leadership laboratory (not mass movement)."

In 1936 the American Association for the Study of Group Work was founded. In 1939 group work appeared for the first time as a separate subject on the program of the National Conference of Social Work. Lindeman saw in group work one of the most promising methods of social work. "A group is a specific form of human interrelation, namely a collection of individuals who are experimenting for the purpose of determining whether their needs are more likely to be satisfied by means of collaboration than through individual effort. I cannot see why, then, groups and group experiences do not stand at the very center of social work's concern." [3] As Mary Richmond had in 1920, he saw the importance of individuals' efforts to work together to solve their problems.

In the beginning group work was practiced mainly in leisure-time agencies, and Lindeman recognized its importance in this context. But to him it signified more than play, as his *Leisure — A National Issue* shows. "To the person who has begun to recognize some of the implications of life in a scientific and technological world freedom means interdependence, collaboration, relatedness. When a person of this type begins to think of recreation or leisure, he will automatically turn his attention to questions of cooperation, release and planning." This meant that the group work method, when used in leisure-time agencies, could consciously aim toward helping people to cooperate, to make decisions, and to improve their mental health.

[3] Lindeman, "Group Work and Education for Democracy," *Proceedings*, National Conference of Social Work, 1939, p. 344.

Lindeman warned against using group discussion or the group work method in a mechanistic way.

This mechanical adaptation of group work is bound to result so long as coaches and recreational leaders are themselves deficient in sociological, psychological and philosophical training. . . . We begin to see, therefore, that recreational leadership is something more than personnel trained to teach children and adults how to play games. This simple and isolated function might be in and of itself useful but it might also become dangerous. It might be preferable to have a child, for example, seek his own way of utilizing leisure than to be submitted to the guidance of a recreation leader who possesses no reasoned philosophy of life.

He emphasized that there was no place in social work for any empty mechanical technique: a technique could be developed only in relation to a basic philosophy of life. Group work was especially suited to a democratic philosophy because of its dual concern with cooperation and with the creativity of each individual within the group. His specific interest in developing the group work method points once more toward his never-ending concern with the goals of social work and the manner in which they could be translated into methods.[4]

Casework — perhaps because of his personal fear of too-intimate contacts — was somewhat beyond his reach. But in the decade of the 1930s he attempted to apply his philosophy to the development of a method of *social research*, an attempt so premature that it unfortunately had little influence on the profession.

This attempt is contained in *Dynamic Research*, written with John J. Hader. Lindeman's concept of social research foretold much of what is being discussed today. He insisted that the methods of social research must necessarily be different from the methods of research in the natural sciences, because values — those of the researcher and those of the people who are objects of the research — are always part of a social situation. One could not, therefore, look for "objective" facts, but had to discover facts and know that they were infused with values. The self-awareness of the researcher was

⁴ Lindeman, *Leisure — A National Issue. Planning for the Leisure of a Democratic People* (New York: Association Press, 1939), pp. 14, 25, 45.

essential. Social work education, in teaching methods of casework and group work, has put great stress on self-awareness for the client; it is essential that the profession recognize that self-awareness is equally important for the researcher. The methods used in social research should be interviewing, investigating records, participant-observing, analyzing situations, and recording situations.

The book was written to develop a methodology of research. The authors' basic philosophy of social research was expressed thus:

1. Our chief purpose in using the adjective "dynamic" is to indicate our belief that social research should somehow be usable as an implement of social change.

2. Certainly it is not enough as some social scientists appear to believe, merely to accumulate studies of isolated phenomena: the sum of parts does not always make a whole.

The latter principle was especially significant for social research, and one which was — and is — not generally accepted. To Lindeman, studying a phenomenon without having a clearly defined purpose and without seeing the phenomenon in the context of a whole situation was unscientific. For this reason his studies were done in real life situations and not in laboratories.

Hader and Lindeman were especially interested in the functioning of joint committees of employer and employees. By observing live practice they began to study the impact of the group on individuals. This was among the first studies into group process, and some of their discoveries are still valid. They found out how, in a given group, the individual acted as representative of another group or some other interest. They realized the importance of the individual's status in the group to the content of his contribution to the group. They established an interesting definition of the group. "For the purposes of psychosocial research the 'group' must be considered as a psychic entity. The use of the fictional term thereby becomes fictional since the collective symbol can only be regarded as a convenience if not a necessity for individual thinking. It is indispensable as a generalized term. However, it must be kept in mind that the essential reality is the individual's response to this fiction and not the existence of the entity as such."

This definition is significant. It denied that the group can have a greater value than an individual. To Lindeman and Hader the individual was the important entity, but they recognized that individuals in interaction may form a psychic unit which influences the behavior of single individuals.

They emphasized the use of a variety of techniques, some enumerated above, in social research. They considered especially important the discussion method which could help to bring out various opinions about social problems. They also recognized the need for statistical techniques, but asked that they be used with caution. "Social statistics . . . are not trustworthy unless the facts enumerated and collated have been examined by some other technique which is qualitatively distinguished from mathematics." [5]

The "wholeness" of the approach to social research and the use of field observation were new; these two concepts influenced social psychology more than social work.

With the 1930s the concern for clarification of the relationship between *private* and *public* welfare grew. Those were the years of the depression and the Roosevelt reforms. A highly individualistic country had difficulty in accepting the need for planning and for government concern for the individual. Lindeman was in the forefront of those who considered planning essential, again using his principle of rejecting "either-or" thinking. To him "dynamic logic" meant that "all situations, as well as all objects, can be arranged in graded series." In the United States this meant that there could be many varieties of capitalism "within the graded series beginning with force, coercion and absolute authority on the one hand, and consent and functional authority on the other." [6]

He became more impatient than ever with a narrow concept of social work as having the exclusive goal of rehabilitation of the unadjusted individual. To him this meant that social workers were not yet dealing with the total situation. "Adjusting related only to status quo. Social work should be a profession whose members are

[5] John J. Hader and Eduard C. Lindeman, *Dynamic Social Research* (New York: Harcourt, 1933), pp. ix–x, 67, 120.

[6] Lindeman, "Planning: An Orderly Method for Social Change," *Annals of the American Academy of Political and Social Sciences,* July 1932, pp. 1, 3.

skilled in conditioning human behavior and who are devoted to the aim of releasing the potentialities of individuals by means which relate them to a changing and dynamic society. . . . Social work . . . would become the instrument of social justice on its lowest level and of social change on its highest." His principles of the continuity of all action and thinking and of the integration of means and ends were expressed in his assertion that social workers could not find unity in their profession if they did not work towards unity in society. "We must relearn the ancient lesson which teaches that we only find freedom for ourselves when we help to set others free." [7]

During the decade of the thirties Lindeman was close to the general problems of social welfare and the specific problems of the young social work profession.

The growing economic depression led him to an intensified inquiry into the basic goals and principles of social work. Justice had to be translated into practice. This meant changing the status quo. It meant government planning and acceptance by the public and by the profession of social work of responsibility for public welfare, while at the same time individual initiative had to be safeguarded.

He did not stand alone among his colleagues in this thinking. Two significant contributions to social work philosophy that appeared at this time were written by persons close to Lindeman; it can therefore be assumed that Lindeman influenced the authors, and they Lindeman. One of these publications was a paper by Antoinette Cannon, a colleague of Lindeman; the other Reinhold Niebuhr's book, first presented as a series of lectures at the New York School, *The Contribution of Religion to Social Work*.

Antoinette Cannon acknowledged that social work had not yet produced a formulated philosophy; she recognized that a major reason for this was social work's concern with pressing daily problems. Social workers therefore tended to take objectives for granted, and focused more attention on the development of technique. Their interest and curiosity about the causes of the problems which they encountered, plus "a passion for exactness" led into scientific inquiry

[7] Lindeman, "Basic Unities in Social Work," *Proceedings*, National Conference of Social Work, 1934, pp. 511, 515.

about human behavior and societal forces. Technique and science "effect their difficult but inevitable union in practice, before there is evolved a theory of the profession as a whole." For the first time a social worker looked upon the dominance of technique neither as a major error nor as a panacea, but simply as an inevitable growth, and she accepted it as such. She recognized the importance of the development of technique and saw that out of this could grow "a system of concepts and values." In her view, the specific interests and values of social workers were (1) relation between individuals and the social scene; (2) relation between individuals and the small group; (3) relation between individuals and the state; (4) relation between individuals and individuals, especially in professional relationship; (5) groups in society (minority groups, race relations, etc.); (6) the value of individuality; (7) the value of subgroups; (8) the value of society; (9) the desirability of the conscious control of society by itself. As an outgrowth of these she postulated a basic idea: "Interdependence . . . rather than independence, as self-help has come to mean the organized effort of a group to satisfy its own needs and not alone the effort of the individual." [8]

This idea of interdependence with emphasis on group efforts was close to Lindeman's teaching and writing during this period, and it was in step with the times. At the same conference Harry Hopkins spoke on the national program of relief and said, "The New Deal is here." [9] The New Deal was a departure from "rugged individualism" to mutual responsibility and an acceptance of self-help by organized groups. Behind the changing outlook surely stood the committees of unemployed and this new attitude led to Section 7 of the National Industrial Recovery Act which gave labor the right to organize.

The acceptance of the philosophy of interdependence had special meaning for the profession of social work itself. It meant that social work should be practiced by public as well as by private agencies. It meant that there should be room for individual initiative as well as

[8] Antoinette Cannon, "Recent Changes in the Philosophy of Social Workers," *Proceedings*, National Conference of Social Work, Detroit, Mich., 1933, pp. 598, 601.

[9] Harry Hopkins, "The National Program of Relief," *Proceedings*, National Conference of Social Work, Detroit, Mich., 1933, p. 70.

planning. It also meant that social work should drop its sharp differentiation between caseworkers and group workers. "Long-standing classifications of social case workers, group workers and community organizers do not present so much philosophical difference as does a sort of 'school of thought' separation which cuts across the three," Antoinette Cannon continued.

The "school of thought" separation she referred to was the controversy regarding the proper functions of private agencies and of public planning. She recognized that the different social work methods had much in common; in this she was far ahead of her time. Next to the value of *interdependence* she posed the value of *flexibility*. She did not name it as such but her speech ended with a call for action, for getting away from status-quo thinking: "The vital spark hates mediocrity and stasis." [10] Here was a close relative of Lindeman's "unity through diversity."

Reinhold Niebuhr's book clearly bore the marks of his re-thinking of societal theories. He described the contribution religion could make to relieve economic suffering. The book also showed the influence of the labor movement and of the socialist, though not the Marxist, viewpoint. Niebuhr's was a courageous book. He cast a critical eye upon the attempts of Protestantism to ameliorate social problems; he was not afraid to urge the need to change the system as well as the individual. He spoke of the limitations of a religiously inspired philanthropy. He did not hesitate to remind his audience of Luther's fight, after the Reformation, to protect the existing order against the revolting peasants.

The most obvious weakness of religion in social action is that it seems always to create a spirit of generosity within terms of a social system without developing an idealism vigorous or astute enough to condemn the social system in the name of a higher justice. Religion, in other words, is more fruitful of philanthropy than of social justice.

He felt that religion too often overlooked injustice in this world by keeping its eyes on the Kingdom of God. He pointed out that this weakness of "social conservatism" was not found in religion alone, but in "all uncritical philanthropy," which had not learned that

[10] Cannon, *op. cit.*, pp. 602, 607.

society had to deal with the basic problem of the distribution of wealth and not only with the alleviation of individual distress. He vigorously attacked those who wanted to rely exclusively on voluntary charity even after the depression had hit America.

On the other hand he cited religions that had understood the necessity for more social justice and had fought for it. He mentioned the eighth-century Prophets of Israel who castigated the rich for not considering the poor. And he pointed out that during the medieval period the monasteries made "a clean break with the injustices of society by creating a fellowship of poverty and love within, and yet outside of, the social order. This type of radicalism did not try to change the order of society, but it did not, at least, accept it nor give it religious justification." Among Protestants he found basic understanding of the need for justice among the Diggers, the Levelers, the Brownists, and the early Quakers. The justification for his call for social justice he found not so much in the history of religious endeavors, as in the precepts of Christianity: "Ideally, religion is the commitment of life to the highest values, conceived as the Will of God. The moral potency of Christ into Christian religion is derived from the fact that He is to the religious imagination the symbol of the best that life can be."

Religion which was not dogmatic or stereotyped, he went on, could have therapeutic as well as a preventive force; social workers, for example, had used religion for improving the mental and spiritual health of individuals. He was sure that religion could also be a source of social health: it could help communities to develop more communal spirit by emphasizing the common purposes of several denominations. He saw strength and a real contribution to social work in the religious approach to those looked upon with contempt by others in society. Social work should combine this dedicated attitude with knowledge derived from science.

A Francis of Assisi among the outcasts, a Father Damian among the lepers, an Albert Schweitzer among the careless children of the primeval forests of Africa, a John Howard among the prisoners of England, a Catholic nun among the Magdalenes of the street, these all bear witness to the power of religion to find the "child of God" in what the world condemns, rejects or despises. It must be admitted that religion is not itself able to provide the detailed knowledge of human motives and of the intricacies of human personality which is necessary to the most helpful treatment of maladjusted individuals. Religion, except in cases where it is expressed through highly gifted individuals who have an intuitive understanding of human character, does not supply what must be derived from the science of psychotherapy. The insights of religion are direct and immediate, but they are frequently impatient, too impatient, with detail. Nor is religion always as ready as it ought to be to borrow resources from science. But it is not impossible to unite the insights of religion of a high type with the knowledge which science imparts.

Niebuhr found this basic relationship between ethics and science characteristic of social work. Pure reason could not choose a goal for life, since "reason in the last analysis is morally neutral." To determine the relationship between values something beyond reason is needed. Behind all the demands for social justice and a full life lay the assumption that life has value. This assumption "is so generally made that its religious character is not usually recognized." In the combination of basic motivation which comes from religion, scientific understanding of human behavior, and technique and action, Niebuhr saw the way to solution of social problems.

The social technician, the community worker, the settlement house resident, and a host of other social workers, have actually developed a technique by which they bring some of the lost neighborliness back into urban life. They meet human need with greater understanding and more effectively than the voluntary helpers of less scientific days. They have evolved a method of making human need vivid to those who do not come into actual contact with it, so that the social agencies of a large city, with their various appeals, serve the purpose, not only of meeting desperate social need, but of humanizing socially detached comfortable people who might otherwise be without any sense of responsibility for their fellowmen.

Niebuhr stressed the responsibility of different groups of society for each other. Strongly influenced by the socialist movement of his time, he discussed the great need for a creative religion that would incorporate the yearnings of the labor movement. He thought that the middle-class person had become too engrossed in himself and in the individual as such and had come to disregard intergroup relations. He feared that religion — and sometimes social work — had come too close to this middle-class preoccupation with the individual alone and had betrayed the common social task: "Men happen to be both individuals and members of social groups."

In summary, Niebuhr's view of religion's contribution to social work contains the following principles: The final ends for which we strive in human life cannot be determined rationally; they are based on the religious value of the respect for life. Man must take responsibility for man not only by helping each other in individual cases of injustice, but also by searching for the deeper causes of misery and injustice. This is where science and religion meet. Man must be willing to re-examine social institutions and to change them if they have not proved helpful. Social work is a large part of this effort.[11]

Niebuhr and Lindeman met during the many hours of discussion of the Inquiry group. The similarity in their thinking at this time is obvious. Niebuhr was clearer in his approach to religion than Lindeman. Lindeman struggled more intensely with the question of the relationship between science and religion, and he came to terms with it only in later years. He was afraid of dogmatism, but he recognized, as Niebuhr did, the social welfare possibilities of religion.

In 1936 class notes, a former student has recorded that Lindeman spoke with great admiration of Thomas Aquinas. He discussed St. Thomas's interpretation of Christianity and his deep understanding of human behavior. He cited Thomas Aquinas as the great thinker who had tried to establish the relationship between the supernatural and the natural worlds and who believed in a social order based on religion, philosophy, and science.

We also find in his notebooks clippings and quotations from Jacques Maritain, the famous Catholic philosopher.

From 1930 to 1940 Lindeman was close to the general concerns of social work. The economic needs of the people were great, while the nation struggled to establish new legislation to alleviate the present suffering and prevent another such economic catastrophe.

[11] Reinhold Niebuhr, *The Contribution of Religion to Social Work* (New York: Columbia University Press, 1932), pp. 19, 29, 30, 35, 65, 69, 79–80, 94.

Lindeman helped clarify the thinking of the profession by stressing the following concepts: (1) planning and individual initiative are not incompatible; (2) adjustment means both individual and social change; (3) integration of means and ends is essential.

He also participated actively in the working out of one social work method — group work. He saw in this method a translation of value principles into reality, as for instance in the integration of individual fulfillment with responsibility for the group and in the practice of freedom of expression in discussion groups.

Lindeman developed important ideas on social research in this time, but they were ignored by the profession.

CHAPTER 8

1940 TO 1953: DEMOCRATIC PROPOSITIONS
AND SOCIAL WORK METHODS

As the years went on, the clarification and explication of the goals of social welfare work became increasingly important to Lindeman. This was apparent in his classroom, where more and more he taught philosophy and its application to the current political scene rather than specific methods of social work.

The events in Nazi Germany and the outbreak of the war showed all too clearly that democracy was not something that could be taken for granted; rather the core of democracy was to be found in the *participation* of citizens in community and government decisions.

Lindeman was convinced that democracies were likely to suffer more from internal weaknesses than from the effect of external enemies. In a speech in 1948 he said that he feared most "Those who no longer understand the nature of the modern world; those who no longer care; those who are confused. . . . When I realize the apathy which accompanies the current national election, the lack of interest in choosing a president and congress then I begin to appreciate why some of our more earnest-minded citizens have become alarmed over lack of citizen participation." His answer to this danger to democracy was that one had to provide more *democratic experiences* for more people. He saw that this was possible through adult education and social group work. Democracy could only be learned through action; it had to be practiced. He hoped to teach a group of citizens "how to conduct community audits, audits which will reveal the status of civil rights in the place where you live. The purpose of these audits is not merely to find out what rights are protected and which are in jeopardy in your community, but rather to lay the foundation for a long-term program of action." [1]

Social group work had, therefore, a wider task than providing leisure-time activities and working with emotional problems. It was responsible in addition for providing meaningful experiences in democracy for its citizens and for accepting citizens' action in behalf of a community. Group work and group discussions could have important meaning for each individual.

Through group talk people come to feel that they have some personal part in what is being decided. . . . A person who has joined with his fellows in curbing the monologist within him and in seeking to arrive at a sense of real agreement with his fellows will carry over into all his contacts some intangible benefit that will sweeten his dealings with others. And a person who is not accustomed to speaking, but under the stimulus of small group discussion, manages to make his contribution to the thinking of the group, will carry over into his daily living a new confidence and sense of worth. [2]

It was during the postwar years that Lindeman became more and more the *philosopher* of social work. This period in his thinking was introduced in 1947 by an article with the significant title "Social Work Matures in a Confused World." In it he raised the question of how social work was prepared to meet the needs of individuals in an age of social, economic, and political uncertainty. He saw two laws working in the development of human institutions, the law of continuity and the law of change. The social worker should be able to distinguish between them and know which to follow at a given time. "We must, in short, be capable of analyzing the causes which produce change and at the same time decide in advance where we want change to take us. This act of the will, this decision concerning desired directions, plunges the observer into the midst of values and compels him to function both as a scientist and as a philosopher at the same time."

[1] Lindeman, "Citizens' Participation," Civil Rights Institute, Town Hall Club, October 22, 1948.

[2] Lindeman, "Let Us Reason Together," New York Adult Education Council Institute, Holyday Hills, Pawling, N.Y., April 30–May 2, 1948, pp. 10, 13.

Social workers had to become professionally mature. Lindeman spelled out the criteria for their maturity.

1. They had to integrate knowledge from different sources.
2. They should be able to adapt to different sponsorship without losing their integrity.
3. They should be able to cooperate genuinely with other professions.
4. They should be ready to be admitted to the university community.
5. Their technical conceptions should be able to be translated into lay language.
6. There should be harmony between goal and method and personal conduct.
7. Social workers should feel social responsibility.
8. They should be capable of adapting to the dynamics of society which includes an intelligent approach to administrative problems.
9. They should merge experience and theory.
10. They should be able to attract undergraduate students of superior intelligence to this field.

And beyond all these criteria was the greatest requirement: that social workers keep their warmth and concern for human beings. They should never become cold scientific observers of society. Social work must be "involved in mankind." [3]

In the *Alumni Newsletter* for the summer of 1948, Lindeman urged the graduates of the School of Social Work to be particularly concerned with the increasingly important issue of civil rights.

As citizen, as humanitarian, as technician and as social scientist the social workers bear a distinct responsibility to the question of civil rights, both with respect to its specific incidents and its comprehensive meaning. I cannot conceive of a bona fide social worker who could remain aloof from this cause and still think of himself as having fulfilled his professional responsibilities, to say nothing of his duties as a citizen.

He related this general demand to a specific problem in social work. In 1948 social workers were being urged to investigate relief clients more thoroughly and a campaign was conducted, especially

---

[3] Lindeman, "Social Work Matures in a Confused World," *The Compass*, XXVIII, January 1947, pp. 3–9.

in the New York area, against so-called chiselers on the public relief rolls. The public's hostility to government relief prompted much of the attack. In the *Newsletter* Lindeman put this incident into the context of the civil rights question.

There is . . . one right which I fervently hope social workers will demand for themselves. This right has to do with that intimate and subtle relationship between the social worker and the recipient of his services. A recurrent pressure appears to arise from politicians, from publicists and from an occasional citizen demanding of the social worker that with each act of service he shall also impose a penalty. The source of this sadistic impulse, this will to hurt the person who needs help, is a problem for psychiatrists. The need to resist this impulse is an imperative for professional social workers. No profession can profess to be serving the interests of human welfare if its functions are performed with punitive intent or even with implied punitive accompaniment. The social worker's task is to bring freedom to the person in need, to reveal to him the methods by which he can free himself of his burden and thus regain his sense of dignity.

Lindeman thought that the United States had gone through a peaceful revolution in moving away from isolationism to internationalism, from rugged individualism to the acceptance of trade unions and social insurance. He realized that this peaceful revolution was not finished and in 1951 especially he was called upon to defend its achievements constantly — especially when they were related to the state's responsibility for its citizens. In his 1951 notebook we find an interesting example of how he used historical perspective to support his arguments. In trying to prove that democracy and the welfare state were not contradictory, he noted that all through the history of the United States the government had come to the aid of citizens. His notations say: Hamilton (protect infant industries); Lincoln (land grant colleges); Horace Mann (public education); Theodore Roosevelt (support of farmers); Herbert Hoover (loans to corporations); Franklin Delano Roosevelt (social security); Robert Taft (housing).

He always tried to evaluate the present in terms of the past and the future. He was aware that his ideas about future trends might be mistaken, but he felt that prediction was part of his responsibility. In 1948 he believed the following to be the most important trends.

1. The growth of the world's population, a larger proportion of the aged, and therefore, less responsibility for youth.

2. With the rise of industry increasing family mobility, fewer close friendship patterns, and more people in the cities with increased loneliness.

3. Increasing use of science and technology leading to automatic controls on the economic forces, more social insecurity, and more leisure for the individual.

4. With a greater amount of citizens employed for wages, a greater need for stable economy and provision for periodic unemployment.

This evaluation was not particularly original, but it was important in its practical application and it showed his constant concern with the general problems of his time.

He used his philosophy and his practical outlook to establish criteria for the evaluation of social agencies. His deep respect for the role of the layman in social work prevented him from falling into the trap (as social workers often do) of disregarding or talking down to board members. He considered it essential for board members to be informed about the goals of agencies and about the latest thinking in social work. He expected the person who joined a board of a social agency to have enough interest and integrity to listen to certain ideas even if he could not thoroughly agree with them. The criteria he developed at an institute given at the Waldorf-Astoria Hotel for evaluation of agencies were outspoken and clear, though not complete.

He pointed out that the task of appraising progress in an agency is always difficult but especially difficult in an age when progress all around is rapid. He asked, therefore, that it be understood that any criterion of progress he suggested could change in time. He brought out five points that contrasted earlier ideas with his suggestions for improvement.

1. Formerly, division of labor and specialization were taken as signs of progress. Yet in recent years questions had been raised about overspecialization in social work agencies. "Is the fractional approach to human problems likely to produce fractionalized person-

alities, segmented communities, are we thus losing sight of organic wholeness?" His suggested tests for overspecialization were

a. Has specialization gone so far as to cause a separation of your agency from other agencies operating in related fields?

b. Has specialization brought about a degree of dehumanization of services?

c. Has specialization made it difficult for your agency to collaborate with other agencies which might meet the needs of your clients, that is rendering services which are not permitted by your stage of specialization?

d. Are there evidences of fractionalization of persons, neighborhoods, communities which are traceable to the functions performed by your agency?

2. Formerly, when a private agency could claim community support because its services were superior to those rendered by a public agency, this was evidence of progress. Lindeman advocated new criteria, based on greater cooperation between the two kinds of agencies in helping the public. The criteria should be the following: "Are the private social agencies moving towards a bona fide partnership with those related public agencies operating in the same area? If so, this may be taken as a sign of progress. Also, are the private agencies giving increased attention to that plus-quality which distinguishes their services? If so, such agencies may be said to be progressing."

3. Formerly, if a private agency could raise its budget though other agencies related to it failed to do so, this was considered progress. The demand of democracy is that there should be no weak units in the pattern of voluntary services because this would jeopardize the whole structure. Varieties of agencies should be welcome. "Those voluntary agencies which are moving toward or preparing to move toward a more cooperative and less expensive method of fund raising are progressing."

4. Formerly, when a private agency increased its professional staff and decreased its volunteer staff, this was called progress. But the democratic ideal requires a relationship between professionals and volunteers with a wide range of capacities.

A modern social agency which is moving towards the orderly recruitment of more volunteers and is thereupon planning to provide these volunteers with appropriate tasks and appropriate training may be said to be progressing. In this connection a qualitative standard is also required. It is not necessarily true that those agencies which utilize volunteers at a maximum are automatically to be placed in the progressive column. What matters here, as in so many similar situations, is not the number of persons involved but rather the quality of work they are permitted to do.

5. Formerly it was considered progressive for agencies to have board members with wealth and prestige, even if they did not function as board members. In a democracy any institution demands participating members. Good board members, therefore, are those who (a) exhibit a high level of responsibility; (b) are representative of the community; (c) are "continuously striving to equip themselves for their responsibilities through various means of education."

In the same practical way as Lindeman evaluated agencies in terms of his philosophy, he applied the criteria of democratic values to the social work profession as a whole. His criteria, phrased as questions, were pointed sharply at the issues with which social work was confronted: (1) Had social work ridded itself of the use of all punitive rewards and punishments? Did it work in a way which helped people keep their self-respect? (2) Had social work removed all policies which tended to permit discrimination on account of color, race, religion or national origin? (3) Did social work operate under voluntary and public, tax-supported auspices? (4) Did social work encourage citizen participation? (5) Did social work use its insights for the purposes of social action? (6) Did social work participate in social planning? [4]

These criteria were a call to duty for social work. Lindeman, who held the principle of the "partial functioning of ideals," understood that social work could not always fulfill all the demands. Yet he expected the profession to strive towards them. "Philosophically and

[4] Lindeman, "Steps toward Evaluating Progress in Private Agencies," 1948 Sixth Annual Board Members' Institute sponsored by the Federation of Protestant Welfare Agencies, Inc., pp. 2, 3, 4, 5, 6.

scientifically social work belongs at the center of the democratic pattern of life." [5]

The visit to India (pp. 69–71) gave Lindeman an opportunity to test philosophy and methods of social work *in another culture*. His report on India summarized his experience and presented at the same time his concept of some parts of social work education.

In India he had fifty-seven students whom he divided into seven discussion groups. His purpose was to acquaint them with various discussion methods so that they could increase their capacity to think for themselves. He also wanted to give them an opportunity to apply his lecture material to Indian conditions. In the beginning the students were incapable of using the discussion method. They argued instead of having a discussion. It was important to Lindeman that they learn the arts of listening to others and of cooperating in solving problems. They learned to function as workshop groups. In his unpublished report on his visit to India, Lindeman pointed with gratification to two documents produced in these workshops which he considered very valuable to social work practice. The two documents were "An observation chart or guide to be used in the study of village life in India" and "A plan and program for introducing parent education in an Indian village."

These two subjects were indicative of Lindeman's wide view of social work. They were related to the needs of Indian social work and its strong component of education and not to the more therapeutic aspects prevalent in American social work. But while the content was important, Lindeman was especially gratified by the way his students began to accept the method.

What was probably of most importance, however, was the fact that they began to see education, not merely as repeating what the teacher had said but rather a process in which they might help each other and make use of their own experiences. Indian education in general is, of course, not based upon this principle. All of these students, graduates of Indian universities, had become inured to the lecture, listening, taking notes system of learning.

[5] Lindeman, "Democracy and Social Work: Inter-Relations, Technical and Philosophical," *Alabama Social Welfare*, State Department of Public Welfare, Montgomery, Ala., June 1949.

In India he also tested his conviction of the need for a special course in philosophy for social workers. In his later years he struggled with the question of whether he should teach philosophy *for* social work or philosophy *of* social work. He was not sure that social work could establish its own philosophy and he was wise enough to recognize that the philosophy of a profession which is so concerned with the wide problems of mankind will inevitably coincide to a great extent with all basic philosophy concerned with human relations. In the report on India Lindeman outlined what he had taught in his philosophy course; the content closely resembled what he taught to American students in similar courses. His skill lay in opening up new questions in the minds of his students and increasing their sensitivity to their own social environment.

This outline is reproduced here. (Incidentally Lindeman mentioned that his course outline, which he had prepared in advance, was altered almost daily.)

I. What is the most fruitful method of learning for graduate students in a professional school?

II. What is social philosophy and what is its relation to training for social work? Under this topic, eugenics, euthenics, economics, law, politics and government, and ideologies were considered from the viewpoint of values.

III. Since the various value-problems involved in the above categories can only be considered in the light of certain facts, it became necessary at this point to enter upon a discussion regarding varieties of knowledge, i.e., that branch of general philosophy known as epistemology. We thereupon discussed (1) knowledge which comes from authority; (2) knowledge which derives from intuitive or mythical sources; (3) empirical knowledge; and (4) rational knowledge.

This was in many ways one of the most fascinating phases of the course because it necessitated discussion of cultural distinctions. The class was very much concerned about statistical knowledge and we departed from our general inquiry to insert an element which might be called "social facts." This actually became a major category and hence should be listed below.

IV. The nature of social facts.

V. Facts for use, or dynamic logic. (After this diversion, we returned to our major exploration of social philosophy.)

VI. Democracy as an ideological pattern in which we discussed (1) democracy as a cluster of "mechanical" ways of resolving conflict; (2) democracy as a set of ideal values; (3) democracy as a set of empirical values.

VII. The courses of value for modern man.

VIII. Facts and values in human relations. This discussion led to a desire on the part of the students to learn more about the psychology of growth and American conceptions of so-called progressive education.

IX. Varieties of understanding.

X. Values and the functions of professional persons.

XI. The group, the neighborhood and the community.

XII. The leader and the expert.

XIII. By request: a synopsis of the lectures I had delivered outside the School.

XIV. A session devoted entirely to questions written in advance by the students.

This is a bare outline of the material covered in the class. Due to India's village problem, considerable time was spent on community organization. Students were asked to spend some of their group time in a reading experiment and reports from this experiment were discussed. Reports from the discussion group were intermittently made to the group as a whole.

This outline indicates Lindeman's emphasis on teaching a non-dogmatic philosophy. He considered it essential to teach philosophy as a separate subject in social work, but he wanted to be sure that the teaching should not become indoctrination. He elaborates this further in a 1950–51 notebook:

Rigid dogmatism has injured humanism . . . the religious conception of human nature is: Individuals are ends not means; Dignity inheres in the individual; All persons are redeemable; All are brothers. Science and religion are two ways to find the truth. Religion makes a contribution by cooperating with other endeavors toward human welfare, teaches lower income groups to give . . . makes social work a warm humane expression of neighborliness and affection, insists on ethical-moral quality in all human relations, helps diminish cynicism about do-gooders, doing good is man's highest privilege. Elevate standards of religious agencies so that they are highest models, create fellowship between professional and laymen, see to it that social progress is related to justice.

This statement demonstrates a significant change from his purely pragmatic period in that Lindeman was relating his nondogmatic attitude to a religious base. He had moved away from his early almost defensive attempt to make religion accord with science and his middle period of denial of religion. He began to conceive of a possible combination of science and religion, as becomes clear in the following quotations.

If humanitarian values coincide with religious values so much the better for religion, so much the better for science.[6]

In 1945 he said:

I am appealing for an extension of science into the moral and social spheres. . . . Science without a humanistic orientation is likely to culminate in moral chaos. Likewise, if the humanistic tradition does not align its affirmations with realistic and scientific facts, it will degenerate into a deadly faith which bears no relation to life. . . . When science becomes more philosophic and philosophy becomes more scientific, then there will be light.[7]

Four years later he was more definite and secure:

The notion that science and philosophy are opposites, irreconcilable antitheses, is so deeply engrained in our cultural habits that the very practitioners of these two disciplines are themselves the chief perpetuators of this myth. . . . Human problems are not scientific and philosophical: they are at one and the same time scientifically philosophical, or philosophically scientific. Every unit of behavior is a complex of ends and means, values and facts, purposes and methods.[8]

The "interrelatedness of all knowledge" [9] and the infusion of facts with values were the basic concepts Lindeman continually brought before social workers. He was not unopposed, as can be seen in the words of one of his colleagues, Philip Klein: "Research can discover, expose, explain and gauge the activating forces in social work. It

---

[6] Lindeman, unpublished notebook, January 1951–October 1951.

[7] Lindeman, "Morality for an Atomic Age," *The New Leader*, Vol. XXVIII, No. 36 (September 8, 1945).

[8] *Science and Philosophy: Sources of Humanitarian Faith in Social Work as Human Relations* (New York: Columbia University Press, 1949), pp. 215–17.

[9] *Mental Hygiene and the Moral Crisis of Our Time* (Austin, Texas: University of Texas, Hogg Foundation, 1952), p. 11.

cannot, and therefore should not, attempt to prove their validity.
. . . The choice of goals, on the other hand, the determination
of acceptable social values, the fixing of ethical and aesthetic aspira-
tions, these are a function of will, even of irresponsible will." [10]

This dualism of facts and values was not acceptable to Lindeman.
In his stress on the "one cloth" of ethical demands and action he was
the spokesman of social work, the profession facetiously called "do-
gooders" which had to learn to accept this term as a badge of honor
rather than an insult. In the last years of his life he tried to make the
profession conscious and proud of its specific task as one of the
guardians of the welfare of people. He found elements helpful in
developing such an attitude in the general social situation as well
as in the scientific development of mental hygiene concepts.

The social situation after World War II showed grave dangers
but also promise. Lindeman was concerned because the world was
still divided spiritually into East and West and because many people
needed much help economically and emotionally. Yet he saw the
beginnings of the disappearance of colonialism and racism. He found
less distinction between urban and rural populations, because of
better communication and of improvement of conditions on the
farms. He believed there was latent power and promise in specialists
if they could work with community leaders.

After having quoted characterizations of our age by Toynbee
(age of trouble, time of ordeal), by psychiatrists (age of anxiety), by
religionists (age of faithlessness), and by moralists (age of corrup-
tion), he wrote in a 1951–53 notebook: "I do not believe our
generation is less moral — but we have lost the sense of being good
— due to loss of faith in the moral system we have inherited. New
orientation needed. In the meantime certain new concepts of value
are being evolved through practice, social welfare, mental hygiene."

His idea of a mature civilization was one that had moved from
uncritical optimism to the acceptance of probable tragedy, from
boastfulness (chauvinistic nationalism) to honest patriotism, from

[10] Philip Klein and Ida C. Merrian, *The Contribution of Research to Social
Work* (New York: American Association of Social Workers, 1948), p. 6.

isolationism to participation in world affairs, and from Utopianism to a realistic concept of progress.

In the United States the threat to civil liberties had increased. To Lindeman the profession of social work, whose task was vigilance for the welfare of people, had to be especially watchful. It should fight the narrow "Americanism" expressed in Senator McCarthy's attitude. "An in-growing selfish democracy is a democracy well on the road to decay." He referred to America's early tradition of freedom and belief in values. A speech at the Welfare Assembly showed clearly Lindeman's turning away from a too-relativistic pragmatism. "All honor to Jefferson — to the man, who, in the concrete pressure of a struggle for national independence by a single people, had the coolness, foresight, and capacity to introduce into a merely revolutionary document an abstract truth, applicable to all men and all times, and so to embalm it there that today and in all coming days it shall be a rebuke and a stumbling block to the very harbingers of reappearing tyranny and oppression." [11]

"Consistency" and "democratic discipline" became key words, spoken with urgency. A climate of repression, suspicion, and unconcern for the dignity of individuals was something one had no right to suffer but must fight. On being nominated for the presidency of the National Conference of Social Work, Lindeman wrote to the profession: "Our generation and the profession of social work in particular, is moving towards issues and contingencies of a most serious nature. . . . Certain latent sadistic impulses will come to the surface." [12] In this serious situation Lindeman hopefully asked of social work that it would not become bitter and defensive but that it would find other ways "consonant with the very principles of social work."

Mental hygiene principles seemed singularly to fuse understanding of the individual with ethical demands. Lindeman accepted this fact only late in his life, but then with an enthusiasm almost naive. In a

[11] Lindeman, "The State of General Welfare," paper given at the Social Welfare Assembly in New York, May 17, 1950, pp. 10, 12.
[12] Lindeman, "The Presidential Word" to the National Conference of Social Work in the *Conference Bulletin of the National Conference of Social Work* (Columbus, Ohio, Summer 1952).

1951 notebook he said that the representatives of the mental health movement made the same demands on human beings as he had made on them in his ethical system.

1. The individual should not constantly look for perfection (Lindeman's concept of the partial functioning of ideals).

2. There should be no false antithesis between the too-high demands of the superego and the capacities of the ego. (This was an expression of the same principle.)

3. There should be no shifting of responsibility (Lindeman's demand for responsibility of each individual).

4. There should be no escape from conflict to contradiction (Lindeman's demand for cooperation).

5. There should be no escape from reality (Lindeman's demand for the inquiring mind).

He agreed with the mental hygiene concept of a healthy personality which is capable of collaboration, feels an inner security, can make decisions on its own, is capable of dissent without resenting the other person, accepts success but does not use others as means, and is willing to experiment with new ideas. In his great enthusiasm for mental hygiene ("It is my conviction that mental hygiene is likely to be our most fruitful resource in the immediate future") which seemed to him the scientific justification for unproved ethical demands, he perhaps made the same mistake that Watson had made (and against which he had warned so often): he confused what is with what should be. Actually the mental hygiene movement itself had taken value concepts produced by centuries of philosophy and had translated them into everyday demands for the human personality. By so doing it had made a step forward toward the practical application of ethical demands but it had not *proved* them. The mental health movement — influenced by the scientific demands of the twentieth century — had only changed the word "value" into the word "health." It had recognized that man's inhumanity to man was not always founded on ill-will but often had its "foundation in a background of ignorance and misconceptions." [13]

[13] Albert Deutsch, *The Mentally Ill in America* (New York: Columbia University Press, 1949), p. vi.

A recognition of this fact made scientific inquiry into individual and group behavior more important, but it was a mistake to assume that knowledge of human behavior alone would motivate people to better action. This scientific knowledge could as easily be used to achieve the opposite of humane ends.

Albert Deutsch's impassioned plea at the end of his book on institutions for delinquents is the plea of a person motivated by ethical or religious fervor and not the product of science.

We must think in terms of better society, of replacing crime-breeding slums with low-rent housing fit for our future citizens to grow up in, of abolishing that social disease we call poverty; of creating more meaningful social values and moral goals than the shoddy ones that possess so many of us in everyday life; of eliminating the racial and religious discriminations that produce anti-social tensions and resentments; of building community interests in terms of the society of the child as well as the society of the adult.[14]

Mental hygiene concepts could not replace ethical demands: "The moral act is a choice between conflicting values." [15] However, mental hygiene concepts together with a clear value system could produce the picture of an integrated and healthy personality.

In the notebook of 1944 Lindeman described what he considered an integrated personality. (Present-day psychiatry and psychology have difficulty in defining health. These notes might make a contribution.) To Lindeman a person was integrated when (1) he could be loyal to the whole of himself and humanity without discrediting parts of it; (2) no "disprivileges" remained in him — the person who was discriminated against could not feel healthy and integrated; (3) he avoided no responsibilities; (4) he enjoyed all immunities and rights that other people enjoyed; (5) he respected cultural values, honored them, and used them.

The 1951 White House Conference on Children and Youth, in which Lindeman participated, arrived at a definition of a healthy personality which related closely to the above concepts, namely the

[14] Albert Deutsch, *Our Rejected Children* (Boston: Little, Brown, 1950), p. 292.

[15] Lindeman, *Mental Hygiene and the Moral Crisis of Our Times* (Austin, Texas, University of Texas, Hogg Foundation, 1952).

importance of harmony in the human being as well as his responsibility toward others.

First and most obviously, we imply that to be happy and responsible is to be healthy in personality. If so unscientific a statement can be allowed at all, it is surely only if the emphasis is on the "and." Many people are apparently happy without being particularly responsible as citizens, and perhaps without being healthy in personality. Many are responsible citizens but clearly far from happy — and certainly not healthy, as their stomach ulcers and even suicide attest. What we desire in these days of strain and crisis is that young people shall have both of these qualities, so that, among other things, they may produce a social order in which the chance for happiness will be greatly improved.

In stating the matter this way we imply, too, that happiness is something other than a lighthearted, frivolous pleasure in one's own well-being. The happiness that characterizes a healthy personality, the happiness that endures in spite of the individual's and society's vicissitudes, is made of sterner stuff. It is an equanimity indicative of personal integrity. It encompasses the possibility of both anger and tears.[16]

With this more integrated view the social work profession moved closer to the acceptance of Lindeman's view. At the same time he was giving greater acceptance to mental hygiene principles. The profession itself also seemed to listen more attentively to the warning against being lost in technique and began to see the need for clarification of its goals.

Lindeman's last book, *The Democratic Way of Life*, added his most significant statement about a value system and presented the cumulative thinking of years. He called his values "propositions," explaining the use of this term as "based on the assumption that what is proposed is action." In the first part of the book his co-author, T. V. Smith, discussed the general ideals of liberty, equality, and fraternity, of which the one most crucial to both authors was equality, because it covered social justice. Lindeman made it his task to translate those ideals into practical propositions which could lead to action. It was important to him that nobody "be deluded

[16] Helen Leland Witmer and Ruth Kotinsky, eds., *Personality in the Making* (New York: Harpers, 1952), pp. xvii–xviii.

into thinking we have performed the act when we have merely repeated the word."

I conceive of ideals as playing this important role: we are informed by our ideals with respect to each step we take in the daily round of life: If these successive steps are consistent, they will carry us towards our ideals. If we desire freedom, then we must move in the direction of freedom-giving experiences. Otherwise we may say freedom is our goal and yet behave in such manner as to make its ultimate defeat inevitable.

No ideal could be worth anything that had no "empirical counterpart."

THE VALUE PROPOSITIONS

Proposition 1: Unity is achieved through the creative use of diversity. Lindeman considered this principle a rule of conduct based on the laws of nature and humanism. In Nature organisms that display a margin of difference survive more readily than those that have a tendency toward uniformity. In human society the right to differ is "the *sine qua non* of freedom and hence the symbol of humaneness in personal relations. The moment one person demands the privilege of shaping others to his image, kindness, generosity and tolerance remove themselves from the equation." Lindeman recognized that absolutism and totalitarianism were simpler concepts than democracy and more easily practiced, and that the practice of this proposition would therefore demand a great deal from the individual. Since diversity is consonant with the rule of nature, the person who strives to make others conform is a sick person. (As we have seen, Lindeman was very much influenced by the mental hygiene concepts of the 1950s. At several other points he equates health and morality.) Pluralism had become embedded in the Constitution of the United States, but it had not yet been put into practice in all spheres. He pointed out that it had not been carried through, for example, with respect to the treatment of the Negro. Religious differences, too, had not always been dealt with according to this principle. And in economics, people too often considered only the two extremes — the thesis of free private enterprise and the antithesis of state-controlled collectivism — and neglected the possibility of a "plural economy" in which "individual private enterprise, corporate enterprise, cooperative enterprise and government operated enterprise would furnish incentive to a wider cross section of the population."

Proposition 2: The partial functioning of ideals. This principle imposed on people a discipline which Lindeman knew was not easily accepted. His insistence on experimentation was consonant with this proposition. To him "the all-or-none principle belongs to dictatorships. Dictators are not permitted to make mistakes, they must be right in every instance. Infallibility is their claim. . . . Democracies, on the other hand, must of necessity postulate a margin for error." Democracy uses the majority vote only as a mechanical device to experiment. "The majority's responsibility is to conduct an experiment under the watchful eye of an alert and critical minority." This principle demands responsibility on the part of the members of the majority as well as the minority. The minority must assent but must continue to understand the issues involved and to work on increasing approximation toward the goal. Most controversies revolve around means rather than ends. For this reason, those who are willing to experiment with different means and methods will come closer to the democratic ideal. "The experimental mood excludes perfectionism and finality."

Proposition 3: Means must be consonant with ends. "Of all the democratic disciplines, this is, alas, the most difficult to teach and apply." Lindeman tried to show that ethical demands were based on science.

The doctrine which holds that ends justify means is not merely immoral but also unscientific. If the problem were submitted to a psychologist, for example, and he were asked to furnish a scientific explanation of the opposite doctrine, namely, the assumption that desirable goals cannot be achieved through the use of undesirable methods, what answer could he give? In the light of experimental knowledge regarding the behavior of organisms he would be obliged to reply: "An organism becomes what it does. Or, a person's character finally takes on the pattern of his acts, not his wishes." If the same question were put to a psychiatrist, he too would be obliged to respond by saying: "Yes, of course, when actions fail to correspond to values, the end-result is a divided personality, and a chronically divided person ultimately becomes a sick person."

We become what we do. From a scientific viewpoint there is no escape from this law, no escape save moral betrayal. How unreasonable and unscientific is the notion that persons who tell lies, who perpetuate dishonest conspiracies and circumvent laws will ever succeed in creating a better world! And how absurd is the accompanying pretext that persons who suppress freedom will thereby conserve it! "The ends pre-exist in the means," said Emerson and so also says science. If humane and liberal ends are desired we must behave humanely and liberally. The citizen who strives for democratic goals must discipline himself in the use of democratic means.

Lindeman's reasoning cannot be proved. Though he quotes psychiatrists who say that the end result of a personality who uses means not in accordance with the ends is a sick person, we have no experimental proof of this. On the contrary, history has known personalities who have achieved their ends by immoral means without an obvious personality breakdown. The twentieth-century observer might call Machiavelli's a sick mind, but this cannot be proved medically.

We must respect Lindeman's constant endeavor to relate scientific understanding to ethical demands but we cannot completely accept his argument. At the same time we must recognize the importance of the proposition as an ethical demand.

In his enlargement of this proposition Lindeman was again very practical. He talked, for instance, about the educators who bear a large share of guilt if "children become end-gainers in and through the educational process." The constant use of examinations must make the child think of education only as a means of passing examinations instead of as an enjoyable end in itself. He argued against those liberals who fight totalitarianism by behaving like totalitarians. He could not believe in the necessity for fighting fire with fire. He took this proposition seriously and knew the difficulty of applying it. His struggle is clear when he discussed the questions of war and democracy in terms of ends and means.

Liberal democracies should be forever on the side of peace, but how can they adhere to this doctrine in a world in which aggressor nations exist? Passive resistance may be an ideal answer to the aggressor, but it is a form of resistance and in the end it engenders violence.

War is a test of survival. When a democratic nation becomes involved in warfare it is compelled to suspend some of the democratic rules. Its diversity is now overshadowed by the urgent need for unity. War substitutes, for the continuing and fluctuating ends of organic life, the single and mechanical end of survival. This is, of course, a harmful experience and a nation constantly on the alert for warlike possibilities, a military nation, cannot long remain democratic. If a nation remains militarized long enough, its democratic habits will wither and die. Here as elsewhere the means will finally determine the ends.

Proposition 4: Genuine consent is a vital ingredient of the democratic way of life. In this proposition Lindeman included the method to achieve such a consent — discussion or conference. He insisted that citizens of democratic societies must acquire the skill of conferring. This meant not only the expression of opinions by individuals, but contribution by each person to common understanding. "Discussion is a circular, not a linear, mode of communication. Linear, or one-way, communication is suitable to dictatorships . . . The purpose of discussion is to exercise one's freedom in arriving at conclusions in collaboration with other free persons." He thought it important that those discussions should not "fall into the trap of false antitheses." Group discussions could help in moving away from the either-or attitude, and allowed for coming to a responsible solution of a problem. "A candid discussion of morals in a group furnishes an antidote for hypocrisy. A single moral principle hammered out in discussion and applied to real situations is worth tons of affirmed values which are never put to an actual test."

Proposition 5: Economic, social, and cultural planning are modern requisites for survival. Lindeman considered planning a necessity especially in a period of technological advancement. Again he fought the either-or reasoning which considered freedom and planning incompatible. He recognized that there were societies which divided the population into two groups, those who did the planning and issued commands and those who carried out the plans and obeyed. But this contradicted the principle of freedom. Yet he saw the possibility of using planning as a means for bringing more and more citizens into participation. In his amplification of this proposition he made very practical suggestions about the way democratic planning could be done. He believed that some of the reconciliation between security and freedom would be made possible by a conscious effort on the part of experts to learn how to collaborate with other experts and with laymen.

Proposition 6: Efficiency for democratic institutions is derived from functional correlation. The principle of diversity allows for differences and, therefore, for conflict. If one held to this principle alone, democratic theory would result in practical chaos. At the same time that it allows for conflict, a democracy must also give its citizens a sense of direction. Citizens of democracies must, therefore, find methods for dealing with conflict. "The health of a democratic society may be measured according to its ability to invent new methods for dealing with a variety of conflicts."

As examples of the incapacity to correlate and to deal with conflict, Lindeman cited the experts who had too often divided the community through their "institutionalism." Instead, he believed, their goal should be a growing relatedness with each other. "Institutional insulation finally leads to functional inefficiency."

The health of the community is based on a complementary relationship of private and public agencies. As an outgrowth of his experience in social work — particularly the surveys he had made in the later years of his life — he said: "Community fund-raising is a democratic gesture. It remains nothing more than a gesture so long as the institutions which profit financially fail to take the next logical step, namely functional correlation."

Proposition 7: Democratic precepts and ways of living must be incorporated in the educational system. This proposition is less a value than an important practical way of making democracy (as a valuable way of life) effective. "The democratic way of life cannot be taught merely through the introduction of various items about democracy. . . . Participation, as Aristotle foresaw long ago, is the *sine qua non* of democratic behavior. . . . it is precisely because democracy admits of difference and disagreement that it requires participation. Participation in arriving at decisions is the method through which citizens of democracies learn the democratic way of life." Once again, he used practical examples in discussing the application of this value in schools, in communities, in youth councils, and in work with college students. "The habit of participation is the most precious possession of a democracy's citizens." [17] These are the values Lindeman spelled out. To him social work was a profession concerned with the totality of human relations and his specific task was to keep this total concern together in the face of much professional specialization. It had to fulfill this task in cooperation with other specialists and, most important and significantly, with all citizens of the human community. Because of this concern with interrelationships social work had constantly to be aware of the values it stood for. Its understanding had to grow out of a disciplined nondogmatic scientific search and out of a deep inquiry into ethical values as they had grown through the centuries.

Its methods represented the combination of scientific knowledge and value-determined goals: "Casework, group work and community organization — are all founded upon the assumption that science can help human beings to lead a better life by applying scientific principles to personal, individual, family, neighborhood and community processes and situations." But "science cannot fulfill itself. It can furnish the means, but not the ends, the instruments, but not the goals, the facts, but not the values." [18]

LINDEMAN'S INFLUENCE ON SOCIAL WORK

Lindeman had not established a new value system or a social work philosophy. He had brought to social work the wealth of the humanities, a deep belief in an inquiring mind, and a persistent call for an awareness of ethical goals. He had helped with working out some of the methods — at least in their beginning stages, but his special interest was the inquiry into the part played by values in the profession and in all human relations. For some time he seemed to be rather alone in this; however, war and postwar problems brought philosophical problems to the fore. From about 1941 on, publica-

---

[17] T. V. Smith and Eduard C. Lindeman, *The Democratic Way of Life*, pp. 45, 110, 111, 112, 113, 118, 119, 120, 123, 126, 127, 129–30, 131–32, 133, 134, 143, 147, 148–49, 151.

[18] Lindeman, "Science and Philosophy: Sources of Humanitarian Faith," pp. 219, 215.

tions related to thinking about social work goals increased. Some of those published during the last decade of Lindeman's life are included here because they present a picture of the growing influence of his thinking.

The major problems raised in these publications concerned individualism and group responsibility, private and public services, helping the individual and helping society to change, interrelationships of subgroups within the profession, and the way in which the dignity of the human being could be safeguarded in the helping process. Depending upon the specific background and beliefs of the author, these values were based either on the demands of a specific religion or on a general secular humanitarian approach. It is noteworthy that there is almost complete agreement between these two approaches in spite of their different origins. Knowing social work practice we realize that this was not always true in the *application* of principles,[19] but this did not become evident in the philosophical writing.

Jane Hoey, in 1941, stressed the importance of moral convictions and asked social work to return to the religious motivation she finds incorporated in the foundation of the government of the United States. Government exists to protect individuals because they are "endowed by their Creator with certain inalienable rights." She deduced from this basic philosophy that social workers had to accept the interest of government in individuals and at the same time they themselves had to be "the watchdog of democracy." [20]

In the forties the philosophical emphasis was more and more on the democratic base of social work. Democracy was in a life-and-death struggle with the Nazis who were overrunning Europe and threatening the whole world. Social workers became aware of the

[19] There was, for instance, a violent disagreement between Catholic Charities of New York City and the other social agencies over the acceptance of the Planned Parenthood Association into the Health and Welfare Council. Each side based its opinion on the same value principles. The Catholic group stressed the dignity of the individual even before it was conceived and the consequent need to protect it. The other group also accepted the value of the dignity of the individual, but emphasized the right of the mother and the family to have a healthy family life.

[20] Jane M. Hoey, "The Contribution of Social Work to Government," *Proceedings*, National Conference of Social Work, 1941, p. 17.

close relation between their own goals and those of a democratic society. Advocating a focus on individual adjustment alone was no longer possible.

Gertrude Wilson's 1942 address to the National Conference referred to "the accomplishment of a social goal conceived in a democratic philosophy." She emphasized that society often denied self-esteem. If we want the individual to be free and to retain his sense of inherent worth we must make conscious efforts to safeguard these qualities. Social group work, which deals predominantly with voluntary associations of individuals, has had this specific function. "The quality of group life is dependent upon the set of values which are dominant ideas of the members and of society as a whole. Group work is a method by which group life is effected with reference to these values." Social group work's task was the difficult one of reconciling in daily practice maximum regard for the rights of each individual with full concern for the rights of all individuals. "We realize that freedom for the individual is not sufficient and that freedom for society is essential if the individual is to be safeguarded." [21]

The concern over the threat to democracy, along with the realization that society's problems were related not only to economic disadvantages but also to problems of restriction of freedom and restriction of opportunity, opened up a much wider task for the profession, gave it a heightened sense of responsibility and an increased desire to search for values and the means of putting them into practice. Hertha Kraus summarized this by saying: "Our basic efforts have always dealt and will always deal with the unending task of helping human beings to live more satisfying and more productive lives within a given society. In a democracy, however, our concern is every human being in need of help, not just the hand-picked few, admitted by highly selective agencies." The practical implications of her demand for democracy were that social workers should be concerned with the outer and inner resources available to men, they should be "dealing systematically with causes of needs instead of

[21] Gertrude Wilson, "Human Needs Pertinent to Group Work Services," *Proceedings*, National Conference of Social Work, 1942, pp. 341, 342.

painful, wasteful results." She called for "socially conscious generalists" whose goal was "building a community fit for man." [22]

Combined concern for the individual as such and as a citizen of the community is shown in the contribution of Gordon Hamilton, a colleague of Lindeman, to *Social Work as Human Relations*. She cited "the great human principle . . . to be found in an evolving concept of democracy, one of the central ideas of which is a deep conviction as to the worth of the individual and belief in his capacity to participate in his own government and destiny." She realized that basic principles might be used in different ways in practice:

The assumptions that define helpfulness and cooperation in the human welfare must have their base in scientific knowledge and human values linked in practice. But practice in any profession is itself an art, and there is room for great diversity and many sorts of cultural adaptations. Common needs persist within cultural variations. . . .

Social work lies midway between the healing and educational professions and draws on the insights of both. It offers both social treatment and psychological education depending on human needs. [23]

Donald Howard gave a definition of social work in 1951 which for the first time explicitly emphasized the goal of integrating different social work methods as well as the goals of amelioration and prevention:

Social work in any country is that discipline distinguished by a characteristic synthesis of philosophy and knowledge, attitudes and skills whose primary responsibility is to assist entire societies, communities, groups and individuals to attain for themselves the highest possible level of well-being, but which when necessary is responsible also for supplying (directly or indirectly) the goods and services essential to the welfare of the individuals and communities concerned. [24]

In 1951, when social work was attacked because it took a stand

[22] Hertha Kraus, "The Future of Social Work: Some Comments on Social Work Function," *The Compass*, Vol. XXIX, No. 1, January 1948, pp. 5, 6–7.

[23] Gordon Hamilton, "Helping People — The Growth of a Profession," in *Social Work as Human Relations* (New York: Columbia University Press, 1949), pp. 3, 4–5.

[24] Donald Howard, "The Common Core of Social Work in Different Countries," *Social Work Journal*, Vol. XXXII, No. 4, October 1951, p. 166.

against publication of names of clients on relief rolls (Several states proposed or even enacted legislation which permitted this to "prevent relief chiseling.") John Kidneigh supported the profession's desire to protect clients' self-respect and pointed out that opposition to such protection was based largely on misconceptions about "human nature." Among the false ideas he cited were the beliefs that man is selfish by nature, that he is completely rational and can therefore be held responsible for all his mistakes, that he is basically lazy and general insurance is therefore ill-advised, and that the individual can be considered separately from the society in which he lives. To him man was "a living creature, a dynamic expression of his society, a complex constellation of many known and unknown factors, alive, in motion, and in interaction with his environment." The common purpose of social work was for "every person to become the self-sufficient, self-respecting, participating and contributing member of society." [25]

While John Kidneigh turned to the public to interpret social work Bertha Reynolds thought it necessary to remind her own colleagues of this basic philosophy: "There is a disturbing implication in this observed tendency of social agencies to move away from the very poor and highly disadvantaged groups in the community, even though we understand why. It is the implication that these groups are a different order of beings, whose existence we can forget if we do not see them." From her experience of social work under the auspices of a labor union she realized that self-respect was closely related to the feeling that one was not set aside as a "receiver" but that one was part of a community in which one was sometimes on the receiving and sometimes on the giving end.

This was a new concept in social work. For years social workers have accepted — and still accept — as inevitable the fact that taking help is painful, but they did not inquire sufficiently into the reasons for this pain. Bertha Reynolds realized that an important factor in lessening or even preventing the shame connected with taking help was this feeling of sharing.

[25] John C. Kidneigh, "People, Problems and Plans," *The Social Service Review*, Vol. XXV, No. 2, June 1951, pp. 184, 185.

Help must be connected with increase, not diminution of self-respect, and it must imply the possibility of a reciprocal relationship of sharing within a group to which both giver and recipient belong. . . .
It does not seem to be painful to most people if there are certain conditions surrounding the source of help and the need for it. It is not hard to take help in a circle in which one feels sure of belonging.
. . . It hurts to feel doubtful of being able to repay at all, and by that means to be again in full status as a giving, as well as receiving member of the group.[26]

It is surprising that in the long history of giving in social work this simple insight of self-respect as related to membership in a group and to reciprocal giving had not been expressed much earlier. It is even more surprising that this important concept is not fully accepted even today.

Father Terence J. Cooke's *Thomistic Philosophy in the Principles of Social Group Work*, published in 1951, investigates social work's goals from the Roman Catholic point of view.[27] He took one of the two methods of social work — group work — and attempted to crystallize its principles and relate them to the Thomistic philosophy which is part of the foundation of Catholicism. His study was a systematic collection of authoritative thinking in the field, by contrast with earlier writings, which expressed largely the views of the authors only.

Cooke interviewed seventeen authorities on social work, approaching them with a schedule of questions with a view to arriving at principles they held in common. At the time he did this no book had been published which made a similar attempt. The principles he developed out of the interviews were as follows.

I. All individuals have common human needs which they seek to satisfy in groups.

II. The primary objective of social group work is the development of the individual by means of the group in which some of these needs

[26] Bertha Capen Reynolds, *Social Work and Social Living* (New York: Citadel Press, 1951), pp. 4, 162, 25.

[27] Mary J. McCormick, in *Diagnostic Casework in the Thomistic Pattern* (New York: Columbia University Press, 1954), finds Thomistic philosophy in agreement with the philosophy underlying social casework. This book is not discussed in detail here because it was published after Lindeman's death.

are satisfied and/or the primary objective of group work is the development of the individual and the group.

III. In social group work, the group work process, the dynamic interaction among the members of the group and the worker and the group is the primary means of personality growth, change and development.

IV. Since social group work operates in a controlled agency setting the group worker is essential to the group work process and he is necessarily one who has knowledge, understanding and skill in the art of helping people relate to and work with each other.

After having worked out these principles Cooke related them to Thomistic philosophy. The first principle stressed the social nature of man. He found that this coincided closely with the Thomistic principle that man was naturally a social animal. The recognition of man as a social being was deepened by the fact that both Thomists and the seventeen authorities agreed that the group worker should help the human being not only to live *with* others, but also *for* others.

Cooke realized that leading group workers at the time did not completely agree. All of them stressed individual and group, but some considered the development of the individual more important, others the development of the group. He found means in Thomistic philosophy to integrate the two viewpoints. "In the social group, the individual good is subordinate to the common good of the group. However, the common good is subordinate to the final good of the human person which is eternal. . . . The primary objective of social group work is the individual and social development of the human person by means of the group."

The core of group work was the dynamic interaction among members of the group and the primary means of changing personalities was the interaction process. According to St. Thomas, human beings could improve themselves through a process of self-development. Social groups such as the family, the church, and voluntary associations could help stimulate this self-development. Thus Thomist philosophy was in accordance with group work's principle of interaction and the demand for self-help. The voluntary aspect important in the philosophy of group work also had its counterpart in the Thomist emphasis on man's becoming a member of the group only if he *wills* to join.

It is especially interesting that the functional concept of leadership which had been worked out in group work theory and which was considered a modern concept of democracy was found by Cooke to have its counterpart in Thomistic philosophy. "According to St. Thomas, leadership is possible for all members and it results from an interplay of many personalities and environmental factors. . . . Philosophically, the role of the social group worker is that of an instrumental efficient cause assisting the self-activity of group members."

This democratic type of leadership seemed to Cooke to be in full accord with Thomistic philosophy which required activating the personality so that he became "free to realize his God-given potentialities." Cooke said that different social work methods should be closely interrelated. "If social work is not casework, plus group work, plus community organization, plus research, these four methods must be interrelated and integrated into a whole." He saw a way of doing this by putting emphasis on the philosophical base of social work. We realize that this resembles closely the demands made by Lindeman and Antoinette Cannon and yet not fulfilled even now.

Cooke pointed out that the social philosophy of St. Thomas had demonstrated that there was no value in life which could take the place of God. It is at this point that those who base social work on humanistic philosophy alone would disagree. It is striking that the difference lies more in the acceptance of a credo (God or ethics) than in the basic approach to human beings. Both agree on the principles of "the dignity of the human person, the perfectibility of human personality, the social nature of man, the person and the common good, the theory of matter and form, and the philosophy of change." [28]

Herbert Bisno's *Philosophy of Social Work* was another attempt to devise a philosophy of social work in a systematic way. Bisno

[28] Terence J. Cooke, *Thomistic Philosophy in the Principle of Group Work* (Washington, D.C.: Catholic University of America Press, 1951), pp. 112–13, 99, 101, 102, 103 (originally written as a dissertation for the National Catholic School of Social Service).

approached the problem from a pragmatic, secular point of view. He examined the practice of social work and extracted from it the principles, concepts, and values which apparently underlay it. He had been a student of Lindeman, who said in his introduction to the book, "He has with unusual audacity made a beginning on the laborious task of building a philosophical foundation for the profession which is destined to play an increasingly significant role in modern life." Some of the values Bisno found in social work were the following: (1) Each individual, by the very fact of his existence is of worth. (2) Human suffering is undesirable and should be prevented, or at least alleviated, whenever possible. (3) There are important differences between individuals and they must be recognized and allowed for. (4) Rejection of the doctrines of "laissez faire" and survival of the fittest. (5) "Socialized individualism" is preferable to "rugged individualism." (6) Everyone has equal rights to social services. (7) Freedom and security are not mutually exclusive. (8) Social work has a dualistic approach (casework and social action). (9) Social work relies on development of insight and help with the environment rather than ordering, forbidding, and exhortation. (10) Social work considers social planning an important part of its responsibility.

Bisno also discussed social work's concepts of man and of society — concepts that determine values. He concluded that "there is a striking divergence between the philosophy of social work and certain crucial philosophical tenets cherished by important elements of the American culture." He saw major differences between the Catholic viewpoint and the viewpoint of social work generally. According to Bisno, for example, a social worker accepts the concept of personality as a unit of mind and body, while the Catholic Church asserts the duality of mind and body. Again, the social worker recognizes that the many factors determining human action make it impossible to put all the responsibility on the individual, whereas the Church must assert the complete freedom of the will and the consequent responsibility of a man for his actions.[29]

Actually there is no agreement among Catholic writers on this

[29] Herbert Bisno, *The Philosophy of Social Work* (Washington, D.C.: Public Affairs Press, 1952), pp. vi, ix, 126.

point. Cooke's work, discussed earlier, Jean Mouroux's *The Meaning of Man*, and Karl Stern's brilliant *The Third Revolution. A Study of Psychiatry and Religion* are recent writings by prominent Catholics which accept the concepts of personality as a whole and many insights derived from psychoanalysis and prove that this is consistent with the teachings of the Catholic Church.

Every principle and value presented by Bisno is accepted by a number of Catholic writers. The difference of opinion lies in theological concepts. Catholic social workers and non-Catholic social workers actually agree on basic ethics and disagree only on the *source* of these ethics.

Lindeman's thinking penetrated social work increasingly after his death. One of his colleagues, Nathan Cohen, gave as the major address at the Social Welfare Conference in 1953, "Eduard C. Lindeman — The Teaching and Philosophy." He summarized not only the contribution which Lindeman made to philosophy but he challenged social work to re-think those values in the light of current practice. The challenge to social work had always been and continued to be, he said, maintaining the balance between wide social reform and intensive work with individuals. Cohen presented Lindeman's concepts of democracy which would help to integrate those two: "Individualism and humanitarianism," he said, must be "redefined within the framework of democracy as a way of life." [30] He presented the following of Lindeman's concepts as helpful toward this integration.

Man does not exist apart from his relationships or the interdependence of man.

Man needs to learn about his rights and responsibilities.

There is a partial functioning of ideals.

There is compatibility between means and ends.

There is diversity in unity.

There is a need for the act of consenting.

Out of these concepts he derived Lindeman's practical demands on social work:

[30] Nathan C. Cohen, "Eduard C. Lindeman — The Teaching and Philosophy," *Social Welfare Forum* (New York: Columbia University Press, 1953), p. ix.

1. Social work should form a partnership with science, but always to remember, that science tells us "what is," but not necessarily "what should be."

2. Social work education should not be indoctrination but should strengthen the power of criticism.

3. Practitioners should be capable of integrating their methods with methods of other professions which deal with related situations.

4. Social work should remember and keep alive the partnership with lay people.

5. Social work should realize the important role of social action.

PART THREE

A Theory of Social Work

"WE CAN also now begin to see all aspects of human life as so many facets of a unitary human nature, instead of having, like our predecessors, to approach the study of Man departmentally, by breaking it up artificially into a number of separate "disciplines": history, sociology, economics, psychology, theology, and the rest. This new possibility of studying human life as a unity ought to enable us to embark on mental voyages of discovery that have hardly been practicable in the past." Arnold J. Toynbee, "The New Opportunity for Historians," (lecture given at the University of Minnesota, November 6, 1955).

CHAPTER 9

INTEGRATION OF VALUE, METHOD, AND KNOWLEDGE

THE word *theory* rather than the word *philosophy* is used by design in the title of this section. It is impossible for one person to establish such a theory, but the following is a modest endeavor to combine the value component of social work with its present view of the individual and the social scene and the way the profession deals with this combination. This is theory.

Eduard Lindeman brought before social work the thinking of the humanities. In his democratic disciplines he tried to translate some of the more general philosophical demands into practical application. He was not completely able to reconcile his humanistic thinking with the clinical orientation of social work. Today it is social work's task to combine the impetus from the early reform movements with the increased understanding now available of the individual human being in his social relationships and environment. As we have seen in the preceding chapters, this has been tried for the whole profession — as in the papers by Miriam Van Waters and Antoinette Cannon, and it has been attempted for specific parts of the profession — as in the outstanding series of articles by Swithun Bowers, O.M.I.[1] In this chapter I will attempt to answer the questions presented in the introduction that recur continually through the history of social work by clarifying the present basic concepts of social work and their value content and by relating them to the methods of social work.

[1] *The Nature and Definition of Social Casework* (New York: Family Service Association of America, 1949).

This is especially difficult and yet perhaps especially rewarding at this time in history, when with every theory we are looking and searching for a far more integrated view of the world than was ever before achieved. For centuries human beings were content with segmented explanations of the universe. The change in thinking occurring in this century is clearly expressed in the quotation from Arnold Toynbee that opens this section.

The old distinctions among the disciplines are beginning to fade, but we have not as yet the words to convey a completely integrated *Weltanschauung*. For instance, we must still talk about the "individual" in his "environment," though we have learned that psychologically these are really not clearly separate but that the individual incorporates into himself much of his environment and that the environment changes according to the individual's approach to it. We know today that almost all phenomena — psychological, physical, and economic — have multiple causes; rarely can we say that one specific cause produces one specific result. This has made scientific experiment — even in the biological and physical sciences — far more difficult than it was when scientists believed that one cause determines one effect. Single-cause theories such as the economic determinism of Marx have been disproved.

This increasing recognition of the wholeness of all existing phenomena places a great burden on the scientist and on the practitioner whose work is based on science. It demands knowledge of all the formerly separate disciplines. A physician recently remarked to me that not so long ago a person trained in medicine needed to know mainly about biology, anatomy, chemistry, and physics, but now it is just as essential that he know some psychology, psychiatry, sociology, and anthropology. History seems to have moved in a large circle since the time of the Middle Ages and the Renaissance. In those centuries universal knowledge was expected of scholars who undertook to investigate any of the phenomena of our earth. The centuries of specialization that followed added to the total of knowledge but separated the disciplines. Now once again such separated and specialized knowledge proves inadequate. Even a physicist should know something about the problems of human relations if he is to have any notion of the results of his research beyond the purely physical consequences.

With the increase in specialized knowledge, no single human being (perhaps with the exception of some genius as yet unknown) will ever be able to encompass all this knowledge. This leads inevitably to the demand for cooperation, exchange of knowledge, and interaction among disciplines. History demonstrates that men have always been interdependent. The interdependence of scientific endeavor is not yet completely accepted by everyone, but it is becoming more and more obvious to those who work in applied professions. Social work has continually tried to base itself on the knowledge of different disciplines and to apply this knowledge to its comprehensive practice. The separateness of these disciplines is one reason why social work has swung so frequently from an extreme emphasis on one area of knowledge to an extreme emphasis on another — from a focus on the environment alone to a preoccupation with the individual alone, for example.

Because of its comprehensiveness and its concern with a large variety of human problems, social work is and can increasingly be a force to achieve integration of knowledge and frames of reference. Social workers have sometimes felt impatient and even inferior because they belonged to a profession which has to borrow from so many disciplines, and which, it seemed to some, did not contribute to basic research. With an increased recognition by everyone of multiple causation and of the interdependence of scientific disciplines, social work can make a very important contribution to increased cooperation among disciplines. Its analysis of practice and method demands a comprehensive view, a view that includes value determination as an important part of its theory and practice.

In trying to develop such an integrated theory of social work as a constellation of value, knowledge, and method one may start with the value component. Two of Lindeman's concepts prove very helpful in clarifying this component of social work practice. The first is the concept of "facts infused with values."

In a seminar a social work student raised the question whether it was right for social workers to advocate desegregation where the

whole community was against it. Was it not one of the basic principles of social work to accept people as they are and therefore must
not the social worker accept the mores of the community as a fact?
Undoubtedly the social worker must know, analyze, and understand
the facts about the community. Yet he is not an observer who enters
situations for the purpose of study alone. His concern is first and
foremost to safeguard the dignity of every human being, and the
right of each individual to fulfill himself to the greatest possible
extent — short of abridging the right of others to do so. Segregation
violates this major value.

The facts presenting themselves to the social worker include
values. He in turn influences those facts with his set of professional
values. What are they? Here a second Lindeman concept enters: the
distinction between *primary* and *secondary* values. The two primary
values of social work are the *dignity and the right of each individual*
to full development of his capacities and the *interdependence of
individuals* and their consequent responsibility toward each other
in the framework of their capacities. This philosophy is a basis of
general democracy and has been translated into political systems.
For social work the acceptance of these primary values means constant use of them in daily practice. All practice must be judged in
terms of the fulfillment of these values. These basic values unite such
seemingly different approaches as that of the secular humanist and
that of the Catholic. Controversy is often based on the confusion of
the *origin* of acceptance of this value with the value itself. For those
who base social work on religion the value is derived from God; for
the humanist, from ethical laws. But actually all social workers
accept these primary values.

A very interesting document in American history combines these
origins. In the Declaration of the Causes and Necessity of Taking up
Arms of July 6, 1775, we read: "But a reverence for our great
Creator, principles of humanity, and the dictates of common sense,
must convince all those who reflect upon the subject, that government was instituted to promote the welfare of mankind . . ."[2]
In this document the value of promoting welfare is seen as originat-

[2] *Journals of the Continental Congress*, W. C. Ford, ed., Vol. 11, pp. 140ff.

ing from God, human principles, and common sense. Social work as a profession must accept these different origins because of the diversity of its background. Both its bases, the religious and the humanistic one, agree on the primary values. Their application will differ depending upon how the facts are viewed. The viewpoint — hence the application — has changed in the course of history because additional facts became known or human society changed. This raises the demand for increased knowledge and objectivity in assessing facts. For instance, as long as science seemed to prove that one race was superior to another it was possible to find human dignity only in those who seemed to be human beings. There is no question that this view is no longer tenable; we now know that every race is equally human and equally dignified.

Though Lindeman recognized these primary values, he emphasized that there should be no "absolutes" underlying social work philosophy. This does not seem consistent. The preceding discussion shows clearly that social work *is* based on *absolute values,* namely the *dignity of the individual* and the *responsibility of the individual for others.* This is recognized by all social workers, as seen in the standards for professional practice accepted in 1951 by the American Association of Social Workers:

1. Firm faith in the dignity, worth and creative power of the individual.

2. Complete belief in his right to hold and express his own opinions and to act upon them, so long as by so doing he does not infringe upon the rights of others.

3. Unswerving conviction of the inherent, inalienable rights of each human being to choose and achieve his own destiny in the framework of a progressive, yet stable, society.[3]

Can this absolute value be scientifically proved or must it remain an axiom? Lindeman contended that there is a continuum of scientific and moral values and that moral values can be scientifically investigated. The close relationship between scientific facts and moral values in human affairs has been demonstrated. Yet until now every attempt to prove the value component scientifically has failed. Those

[3] *Standards for the Professional Practice of Social Work* (New York: American Association of Social Workers, 1951).

whose theories of social work derive the moral law from God do not need and will not search for scientific proof of it. Those who base it on human ethical demands will continue searching for it.

I myself consider it sufficient for the profession to accept these basic values, just as mathematicians have accepted axioms and build on them. However, I would welcome any further attempt at inquiry into the use and effect of these values. Philip Klein's complete rejection of the possibility of research into values and Lindeman's conviction that one can extend science into the moral and social spheres are both dogmatic contentions. Integration lies in admitting that the profession is acting on absolute moral values, that we have not yet been able to prove these values scientifically, but that we will allow inquiry into them.

While social workers do agree on the basic values that guide their work, they often disagree violently about the secondary values. For instance, should every woman stay home and take care of her children or should she be allowed to work if she wants to? Is it preferable to have groups composed only of members of the same church or economic status or should they intermingle? Is the use of rewards compatible with good practice or does it lead to too much competition? Should shelter be offered to anyone asking for it or should everyone who asks for shelter be required to discuss his problems with the social worker? Should adoptions be regulated by the religion of the natural mother or the opportunity for any child to have a family?

The defenders of opposite points of view still adhere to the primary values of the dignity of the human being and of human interdependence. They differ over secondary values because of the influence of four factors: (1) their own cultural and family background; (2) the precepts and demands of given groups to which they belong — church, professional, or social; (3) personal experience — illness, abandonment by a significant person, death; (4) different scientific theories regarding human behavior.

All four of these determinants of secondary values lie more in the field of insight and scientific endeavor than do the primary values. Thus secondary values need not be accepted as axioms, but can be investigated. If social work accepts itself as a profession based on primary values which are axioms as well as a profession constantly guided by secondary values which must be investigated, many of the controversies will lose some of their religious fervor and social work will enter a period far more consonant with the calm and cooperative effort expected of a human relations profession.

In what follows I will enlarge on each of the determinants influencing the secondary values. In discussing the fourth one we are moving into an integrated attempt at a theory of knowledge of social work.

1. Cultural and family background. Dynamic psychiatry has taught us that all of us at first incorporate the values of those with whom we identify, usually our parents. Since this happens early in life the influence of these identifications is ordinarily the strongest and most lasting one. This is not to deny that the growing child and even the adult continue to modify these values and attitudes through (1) identification with other persons; (2) consideration of ideas encountered in reading, discussion, and the like; and (3) insight into themselves.

Since one of the profession's requirements is that the social worker be able to understand and accept people with different value orientations, social work education must use all three of the above methods of modifying rigid childhood value systems. In practice today social work uses mostly the second and third methods. For example, the insights offered by anthropology and sociology have helped in understanding differing values in different cultures and economic strata. Social workers, who often come from the middle class (this is changing in recent years), with set middle-class values, are helped to realize that these are not necessarily universal or even the best values. The hardworking husband and wife, for instance — who not only find it necessary to work but who feel pride in providing together for the support of their children, transmit this pride to their children, and give them warmth and companionship in the times they are with them — might teach a middle-class social worker that the "working mother" is not in itself necessarily an evil.

In supervised field work the student is constantly required to gain some insight into his own defenses and rationalizations. For example, if he condemns adolescents because they are too superficial and too eager for adventure, he will be required to look into himself and find whether the determinant of his attitude is perhaps fear of those adventures because he has unconsciously repressed them as being "all bad." Or the student who shies away from admitting any competitive feeling because competition is "bad" might learn through introspection that he actually feels very competitive but has never accepted the feeling as a part of human nature — a part which can be disciplined only when it is recognized.

Social work believes in the possibility of conscious change, which means modifications of value systems. The concept of acceptance is one of the tools for achieving such change. Acceptance means that one does not blame a person for his behavior or for his thinking but rather works with him as a person with innate dignity — regardless of his attitude or his potential for change. Acceptance does not mean condonement. The accepting person has values which at times differ from those of the client or group member. If the client or group member disregards the dignity of others, the social worker's acceptance of him often helps him change and come to respect others.

2. Precepts and demands of a given group. In recent years studies have shown that groups have a very strong influence on individuals. The strongest influences come from the primary group — the family — as discussed above. Secondary groups are friendship groups or any group to which the individual belongs by virtue of his own decision or by tradition. As he grows older such groups become more and more important to him. The groups develop their own precepts and subcultures, with which the individual must conform or leave the group. Some secondary groups demand more conformity than others. Some incorporate unwritten laws which are only implied in behavior — for example the teen-age group to which a youngster can belong only if he shows disdain for school and learning. This is not incorporated in the statutes of the group but it is an iron-clad law for behavior and it determines values. Other groups develop written rules. The ethical codes of professional organizations prescribe value-determined behavior for their members. Each religion has its code of ethics by means of which it aims to regulate the behavior of its members.

Every human being belongs to a number of groups. The adult usually chooses groups whose values can be reconciled or at least are not in too obvious contradiction. For the social worker this means an investigation of the precepts and value systems of the various groups he belongs to. If he finds too great clashes, even among secondary values, he will have to choose whether to stay in the profession or to stay with a particular group. The decision will be most difficult when the social worker belongs to groups whose demands are very specific. This applies, for instance, to the Roman Catholic social worker, whose church prescribes detailed rules for human conduct. The Church considers invalid the remarriage of a divorced person whose first marriage was blessed by the Church. If a Catholic couple comes to the Catholic social worker with a marital problem or to work out some problem related to their children, the social worker finds himself torn between the ethical code of his profession which requires him to "accept the right of persons served to make their own decisions and to act for themselves unless they freely give this authority to the agency or unless the agency must act in a protective role in order to safeguard the persons served or the community," [4] and the precepts of his Church which does not admit the right of these people to make their own decision regarding the marriage. Here is a clash of values directly related to practice which seems irreconcilable to many practitioners. Distinguishing clearly between primary and secondary values is of help in solving this conflict. The Catholic social worker can respect the initial right of his client to make decisions — not in regard to his marriage, but in regard to whether he wants service from a Catholic-oriented agency or not. If the worker presents the dilemma to the client openly and without blame, the client can decide whether he will accept the conditions and thereby "freely give his authority to the agency," or will not accept the Catholic orientation and will ask for the services of another agency. By having frankly confronted the client with this

---

[4] *Standards for the Professional Practice of Social Work* (New York: American Association of Social Workers, 1951), p. 5.

choice, the worker has safeguarded the client's dignity. He would violate it if he kept the client in the dark about the dilemma and through insidious pressure forced him in the direction he wanted him to go.

As the foregoing example shows, secondary values derived from group associations cannot be taken lightly and are not always easy to reconcile. At times thinking through these values in relation to the primary ones might change their application. In other instances there will be continued difference in practice which can be tolerated as long as it does not violate the dignity of the individual client or member. Practice must be changed if it comes too close to such a violation or else the worker must choose between his profession and the demands of other groups.

3. Personal experience. Life experience strongly influences the value system of every human being. The more diversified such experiences are the more open the person usually becomes to accepting people with differing value systems. This is one of the reasons why many social work educators consider varied life experiences an important criterion for the maturity and potential helpfulness of a person. A social worker who has never left his own home town and who knows only the values of his economic group and neighborhood will have great difficulty in accepting values of people in a foreign country or even in another part of the United States.

Without question significant events have a strong influence on our value systems. For example, a social worker who had grown up in a rigid orphanage atmosphere insisted heatedly that all institutional placement is damaging to children and that the only helpful placement is in a family. Her own unhappy experience had caused her to believe that institutional placement of any kind was bad. Similarly, a young social worker who had spent the earliest years of his life in a rural area had had a very painful experience upon moving into a large eastern city where he was treated as inferior. He insisted that city life was bad and that there should be a movement back to the farms.

Such examples could be multiplied indefinitely. They show the tendency of human beings to generalize from significant events in their lives and translate them into value systems. The only way to counteract this is to help the individual to gain insight into himself. The concept of self-knowledge and the assumption that most individuals are capable of self-knowledge play an important role in social work education and are expressed in the practice of field work supervision. Modification of values derived from significant life experiences is brought about by self-knowledge and by interaction with an understanding and·accepting person, as well as by new and different experiences.

4. *Different scientific theories regarding human behavior.* This area shows the need of a constant search for a more integrated theory derived from several disciplines and blended into one. At a meeting in April 1956 sponsored by the research section of the National Association of Social Workers and the McCormick Foundation and held in Chicago, several selected research experts in social work tried to develop such a theory during an evening discussion. Clearly, they found, such a theory is not yet available. It might be interesting to repeat here some of the parts of theory which were tried out; I will add my own attempt at integration.

It was brought out that social work in general sees the human being as described by Freudian psychoanalytic theory but omits the concepts of the life and death wishes which were biologically oriented to a high degree. It places more emphasis on understanding the ego, which is relatively independent of the id. Social work sees the individual in unceasing interaction with external reality. It knows the importance of the "role theory," which has made clear that people change according to what is expected of them or what they think is expected of them. Social work views life largely as a constant adaptation to stress and an attempt on the part of the individual to maintain an equilibrium between internal and external pressures. It accepts the possibility of choice, but it recognizes that choices are not completely unrelated to outer circumstances and inner forces. It does not think that each individual makes choices only for his personal comfort — it believes that there is such a thing as an altruistic choice. We have not as yet found the key to the mastering of reality which helps some individuals to stand up under stress even under very unfavorable circumstances. While social work is increasingly cognizant of the human being's capacity to make rational choices, it also acknowledges the role of unconscious drives and conflicts in motivating him.

Social work is aware of the importance of the social control that comes from various reference groups (Lindeman's "vital interest groups"). It takes into account the pressure of the group behavior of the larger environment — that is, cultural influences. Finally, it recognizes that while the individual is strongly influenced by these forces, he is also a factor in changing society.

The Chicago meeting acknowledged that this concept of man had come from many disciplines and that it would not be satisfactory to every social worker. But the experts gathered there agreed that it was a step away from a one-sided theory based on a single discipline, and that it therefore was more applicable to social work practice.

They also agreed that allowing the concept of choice to enter into the theory introduced the value component into the system. They were aware that at the present stage of development there are differences within the social work profession in regard to the concept of the individual in his environment. Some theories put more stress on individual dynamics, others on sociological components. In spite of this, I think that there are some basic theoretical concepts which influence social work practice and which point toward more unity than diversity:

1. Basic to social work practice is the concept of the *capacity for growth and change*. This is not the invention of social work: it was the great contribution of Darwinian theory to the twentieth century. Translated into practice, this concept demands the value of self-determination in regard to the individual and groups. It would have no meaning if it were not given content and purpose — growth toward what and change for what? It therefore forces social work into a clarification of goals, and it must be "an end desired" as Swithun Bowers aptly put it.[5] The concept of the capacity to grow and change is inseparable from the value of the end.

[5] Swithun Bowers, O.M.I., "The Nature and Definition of Social Casework," *Journal of Social Casework*, 1949.

Differently phrased, this value will be the basic one of the dignity of each man and his opportunity to fulfill his purpose so far as is commensurate with allowing this dignity and opportunity to everyone else. It will point to immediate ends — for example, better housing, or integration of the American Indian into our present society without violating his dignity, or helping a rejected child to regain his sense of security and worth, or allowing a group of adolescents freedom to discuss some of their thoughts which seem to contradict their elders' teaching.

2. Another basic concept is the awareness of *the individual as an interacting member* of society and the importance of interaction, individually and in groups, for his development and for the development of society. This concept is the basis of social work's stress on its major tool, the establishment of relationships with clients and members of groups. Interaction includes more than superficial conversations: it is a constant acting and reacting, producing continual change in each individual. Social work sees this phenomenon occurring all through human life. Its professional task is to change this phenomenon, when necessary, into a conscious goal-directed process. Bowers' definition of casework stresses this skill in relationship and combines it with goal determination. He says, "Social casework is an art in which knowledge of the science of human relations and skill in relationship are used to mobilize capacities in the individual and resources in the community appropriate for better adjustment between the client and all or any part of his total environment." [6] This goal-directed relationship is expressed in the definition of the social group worker's function: "The group worker enables various types of groups to function in such a way that both group interaction and program activity contribute to the growth of the individual and the achievement of desirable social goals." [7] And for community organization it is expressed as "the process of bringing about and maintaining a progressively more effective adjustment between

[6] *Ibid.*, p. 19.
[7] Grace Longwell Coyle, "Social Group Work," *Social Work Yearbook, 1954* (New York: American Association of Social Workers, 1954), p. 480.

social welfare resources and social welfare needs within a geographic area or functional field." [8]

Because of the value determination of social work, relationships must not be used to manipulate the individual for the purpose of the social worker. This is probably most explicit in the group work definition:

The objectives of the group worker include provision for personal growth according to the individual's capacity and need, the adjustment of the individual to other persons, to groups and to society, and the motivation of the individual toward the improvement of society, the recognition by the individual of his own rights, limitations and abilities as well as his acceptance of the rights, abilities, and differences of others.[9]

In the light of all this, it becomes apparent that social work cannot be a "nondirective" profession; it is directed constantly toward the fulfillment or approximation of its primary values. But because of these values its methods must combine directiveness with self-determination, which is another basic concept of social work.

Self-determination implies not only a value demand but also a concept of the human being as capable of self-determination. This concept has changed in the course of centuries and there are still psychologic and theological controversies over it. The controversy appeared in the Middle Ages between Lutheran Protestantism and the Catholic concept of Free Will. Economic determinism seemed to wipe out any concept of self-determination, but even Marx was not consistent in his application of this; the action he called for required individual decision-making.

In the early years of social work the notion that heredity determines the life of individuals contradicted the view of the pauper as responsible for his fate. It seems to me that all through the history of human thought deterministic theories have never been held with complete consistency and have always left loopholes for some free choice. In the course of social work's history, on the other hand, the

[8] C. F. McNeil, "Community Organization for Social Welfare," *Social Work Yearbook, 1951* (New York: American Association of Social Workers), p. 123.

[9] Coyle, *op. cit.*, p. 480.

concept of self-determination has been held too absolutely; the power of circumstances was overlooked, and it was assumed that human beings could make their choices with complete independence. Voltaire debunked this in a most delightful way in *Candide*:

At the court martial he was graciously permitted to choose between being flogged thirty-six times by the whole regiment or having twelve bullets in his brain. It was useless to declare his belief in Free Will and say he wanted neither: he had to make his choice. So, exercising that divine gift called Liberty, he decided to run the gauntlet thirty-six times. . . .

Apparently we have reached a more integrated view today. It is clear that no human being is independent of circumstances, of his own inner forces, or of the people around him. Choice, therefore, is never completely free.

The social worker knows that his own self-determination is limited by agency procedures, by his need to make a living, by responsibilities toward his family and toward his client; but he also knows that he can and must make individual decisions when it comes to alternate choices. He will make these choices by measuring the facts as he sees them, on grounds of environmental pressures, of group associations, but also on grounds of his own capacity to reject those considerations if he considers them contradictory to his basic ethical values.

Social workers in Nazi Germany had to make such decisions under great pressure from their environment and from the law of the land in which they practiced, when they were asked to administer Nazi law. They could not disregard the consequences, but they had a choice between accepting practice under the circumstances or refusing it and taking the consequences. This self-determination in spite of pressure was made possible by a firm but not dogmatic belief in the primary values and a constant and conscious exercise in applying them to real situations.

In recent publicity about training soldiers to withstand indoctrination, the opinion has been advanced that putting the soldier through severe tests of frustration and actual hardships would enhance this capacity. In my opinion, such exercise in enduring pain is worthless and bears no relation to the capacity of the individual to make free choices and withstand frustration. In the thousands of unfortunate experiments that humanity has been able to make by the vicious use of persecution, it has had an opportunity to observe that many people who were frail and who had not lived through great hardships did withstand pressure and even torture. Help came from their firm belief in basic values. It is generally accepted in social work that there is such a capacity in the human being even if the source of it is not completely known.

One of social work's basic views of the human being is his need for and dependence on other human beings, the concept of *interdependence*. The importance of group association is recognized more and more. A young and intelligent member of a group of patients released from mental hospitals said that nothing in life was worse than to suffer loneliness. There was not one member of the group that would contradict this. It is true that there have been human beings who have voluntarily renounced communication with other human beings, but this is rare and usually the hermit, too, populates his life with imaginary companions or with other creatures of nature. The group is a most essential part of human life.

Freud described stages of development of the individual human being. Erik Erikson, building on these, enlarged them by taking into consideration the interaction of the child with other human beings besides his parents. The first year of a child's life serves to establish a *sense of trust*. This trust is developed through the relationship with the mother or a mother substitute. The next stage is the development of the *sense of autonomy*. It grows partly out of the biological development of the child and partly out of the child's attempt to learn about the boundaries of self-determination. The third stage is marked by the *sense of initiative*: the child of four or five tries out what he can do. In this stage of development the child works out by experience the interaction between his own desires and those of others. The fourth stage Erikson calls the *sense of industry*, meaning that in this period — around the sixth year — the child wants to engage in real tasks, wants to feel accomplishment, and acquires a sense of duty. Again this is achieved through relation to others.

Erikson sees in the adolescent period the major development of the *sense of identity* — the search to clarify who one is, what role one should play in society. If this sense of identity is achieved or at least approximately achieved the human being then enters a period with most intense emphasis on the *sense of intimacy*. It is the time of relationship between the sexes, of courtship and marriage. The next period is the period of the *parental sense*. This means not only biological parenthood but adulthood, which develops creativity and productivity. He sees the final development of human personality in the integration of all the periods and the development of what he calls the *sense of integrity*.

Integrity thus means a new and different love of one's parents free of the wish that they should have been different, and an acceptance of the fact that one's life is one's own responsibility. It is a sense of comradeship with men and women of distant times and of different pursuits, who have created orders and objects and sayings conveying human dignity and love. Although aware of the relativity of all the various life styles that have given meaning to human striving, the possessor of integrity is ready to defend the dignity of his own life style against all physical and economic threats. For he knows that, for him, all human dignity stands or falls with the one style of integrity of which he partakes.[10]

Erikson's developmental theory has been described here in some detail because it is one of the first attempts to relate Freudian concepts to healthy personality and to integrate them with our increasing awareness of interaction. It also incorporates the value of human dignity into the developmental cycle. Judging from the present-day practice of social work this is probably the personality theory closest to it.

Related to this theory is social work's assumption — expressed particularly in social group work — of society as a network of group associations which have great impact on the individual and which allow for the individual's impact on society. Those group associations vary and change in the course of individual lives. Social work

[10] Erik Erikson, "Growth and Crisis of the 'Healthy Personality,'" *Problems of Infancy and Childhood*, Supplement II, Josiah Macy, Jr. Foundation, p. 55.

practice is based on the awareness of three kinds of groups: (1) the groups into which the individual is born — the family, the nation, the community; (2) the freely chosen friendship groups, and (3) the vital interest groups.

The individual finds fulfillment of his needs in all three kinds of groups, but they have different importance at different stages of his life. The family plays the most important role in early life and the relationships of the very young child are close relationships mostly between the child and the parents. Friendship groups begin to play their part around the early school age. They are usually rather diffuse; the children collect in comparatively large numbers and friendships change frequently. Choice of friends is mostly determined by such accidental circumstances as living close together or meeting frequently or going to school together. Conscious choice of group association becomes strongest in adolescence. This is the time when friendship groups and vital interest groups begin to merge. The adolescent group is usually closely bound by strong feelings for each other, but it also fulfills many specific purposes — athletics, social purposes, or pure security-giving. With increasing maturity, friendship groups and vital interest groups separate, though sometimes the same personalities may be involved. The adult belongs to many voluntary group associations with different purposes — unions, professional associations, political groups, civic associations, and the like. In addition to these, he enjoys a newly chosen family which is no longer the family into which he was born. He also finds friendships according to individual preference.

This *understanding of group needs and purposes* is as essential to social work practice as knowledge of the individual. It serves the therapeutic as well as the educational and social action intent of social work. Through his interest in group work and community organization Lindeman contributed to increased awareness on the part of social workers of their responsibility to work with healthy groups, to increase their interest in and their capacity to establish conditions conducive to the dignity of every human being. He recognized that group discussion and group interaction must be practiced in order to prevent individuals from abdicating their rights to a dictator and from being completely swayed by purely emotional appeals. He saw the importance of working toward creative group association to enhance the enjoyment — not only the usefulness — of voluntary associations so that they become cultural cells of a unified and growing democracy. He stressed the role of the social worker in keeping alive in those associations the concept of the right to differ so that unity should not become conformity. His was a contribution to the educational and action intent of social work.

He did not take part in working out the understanding of groups as a therapeutic medium. This has been added in recent years in social group work and is based more on the understanding of the primary family group and the friendship groups, which give emotional satisfaction to the individual and allow him to overcome feelings of isolation and rejection. Therapeutic group work is based on the same concepts, theories, and values that all social group work is based on, but its emphasis is more on the help the individual receives through group relations and the impact of the worker and less on the action of the group as an entity.

From the foregoing theoretical consideration it becomes clear that the scientific part of social work's basis has come from many disciplines and is becoming more integrated. This scientific part has led and will increasingly lead to *generalization* concerning understanding of individuals in their relationships and of societal structure. The value-directed part of social work is the part that points toward the importance of *individualization* in spite of generalized theoretical assumption and toward an increased amount of responsibility for safeguarding and enhancing an individual's dignity as part of an *interdependent community*. Social work methods, therefore, must continually include both the scientific and the value components. They will be specific in their techniques and skills, but their basic principles will be increasingly seen as common to all social work methods. Some of the principles common to casework, group work, and community organization are as follows:

1. The social worker's goal is to enable clients or group members or groups as a whole to move toward greater independence and capacity for self-help.

2. The social worker must use the scientific method to prepare for action: fact-finding (observation), analysis, and diagnosis in relation to the individual, the group, and the social environment.

3. The social worker must form purposeful relationships: this means a conscious focusing on the needs of his clients, group members, and communities; on their avowed purpose in coming for help; and on the implied — sometimes not fully conscious — purpose.

4. The social worker must use himself consciously. This includes self-knowledge and discipline in relationships, but without the loss of warmth and spontaneity.

5. The social worker must understand the origins of his own value system and be able to handle it in relation to the value systems of others.

6. The social worker must accept people as they are, without condoning all their behavior. This involves deep understanding of his clients or group members as well as knowledge and identification of values regulating human society.

7. The social worker must allow people to develop at their own pace and to choose their own point of departure without immediately imposing outside demands. However, he has a responsibility for stimulating change.

8. Because of his infinite respect for the individual every social worker must help each individual to feel that he is an important and unique person who can contribute in some measure to the whole of society or to a part of it.

Having clarified these principles and adduced the facts and values that underlie them, we can attempt to answer the questions raised in the Introduction.

1. Is social work palliative only or is it responsible also for changing social institutions? The answer must be that social work is responsible for attempting both: to help individuals in the framework of existing conditions as well as to help change social institutions. When we recognize the multiple causation of problems and realize that the causes lie neither exclusively in the individual nor in the societal structure, it becomes clear that a profession which works toward social justice in a wide sense must feel responsible for amelioration and social change. On the way toward these goals social work must consider its means. Because of the values of individualization and acceptance, social work is bound to use methods which take into account the feelings and the rights of each individual even if such methods do not achieve the final goal as quickly as some others might. This distinguishes social work's methods from the methods used in power politics. (I do not want to imply that only social work's methods are good and that others are bad; power politics can be important and justified.) As a profession it must adhere to the principle of the compatibility of means and ends. Its interest in method is therefore justified as long as the methods are clearly related to the goals of the profession.

2. *What is the definition of the needs and rights of human beings?* Social work's answer to this question is based partly on the latest scientific knowledge and partly on the inherent value of the dignity of every human being. Human rights clearly inhere in Lindeman's fourth democratic proposition, "Genuine consent is a vital ingredient of the democratic way of life." This principle separates the Poor-Law concept of social work from the thinking that requires the participation of clients and members of groups.

It is far more difficult to agree on the definition of needs. There is worldwide agreement that humans have a right to food, clothing, and shelter, but beyond this there is no agreement — and in some countries even these basic needs have not been recognized as a right for all social and racial groups. As a society becomes more complicated and as the standard of living rises, other things become essential too. We have acknowledged that the human being needs more than food, clothing, and shelter to come to his fullest development; today we add the basic needs for love, security, knowledge, beauty, work, and varied experiences, as well as the individual's need to belong to something beyond himself. It is quite possible that with increased understanding of the human being we will find more needs. Since social work is concerned with the totality of providing for human needs it has a responsibility to work toward their fulfillment, to restore opportunities where they have been denied to individuals or groups, and to prevent such denial if it threatens. This applies to the individual case of a neglected child, as well as to the case of a whole racial population of a community when it is treated as inferior.

3. What is the theory of "adjustment" in relation to social work philosophy? This question is closely related to the first one — whether social work is concerned only with individual adjustment or also with the adjustment of environmental forces to individual needs. And the answer is the same as to the first question: social work is responsible for the individual's adjustment to existing circumstances, but also for trying to help change social institutions and to help others to find the strength to participate in this effort.

4. What are social work's specific methods in relation to its value system? This question is an especially crucial one because of social work's intense efforts to establish suitable methods. I have said above that this concern with method is an important and justifiable one because of the interrelatedness of means and ends. There is another justification for this concern: a profession which has as its major tool the disciplined selves of its practitioners needs to be precise and careful about its methods. The principles basic to all three social work methods are clearly value-determined. They therefore cannot be taught or learned as simple techniques. Whatever method is used predominantly by a social worker, he must continually be aware of his responsibility for interdependence as well as for individualization. For instance, to deal with the distress of unmarried mothers caused by the punishing attitude of society toward them, a caseworker uses social work methods to help the individual unmarried mother to stand up under the strain; to awaken in the unmarried mother a sense of self-worth; to work at changing society's attitudes toward unmarried mothers.

The group worker who works with a group of epileptic patients uses individual and group processes to help the persons in this group to withstand the prejudice they meet in society and to change legislation covering epileptics. In community organization the goal of the social worker is to improve and increase community understanding, community planning, and community participation in welfare services. Because of the basic values they hold, social workers have no right to reach those goals by manipulation or by hidden use of power groups. Their methods must be governed by a respect for the dignity of those citizens who contribute to services as well as those served. Just as a client must not be left in the dark about the purpose and goal of the agency to which he has come for help, the contributing citizen must be informed about purposes and goals of welfare services.

Social work methods must be evaluated on the basis of their effect on the specific goal for which each is used, and in terms of their conformity with social work's basic values.

If, for instance, because of its respect for the individual, social work stands for *mutual giving* as a human value, then unilateral relationships must be considered poor practice.

If social work considers the *human being as a whole and its inter-relationship with society* as an important part of its dignity then the sharp separation of the individual approach and the group approach in social work must be considered poor practice.

If social work has a *respect for all people regardless of their back-ground*, then manipulation of board members must be rejected as poor practice.

If social work recognizes *individual differences* as a value, then stereotyping or pressing people into a mold is poor practice. This would apply to social group work when members are forced or persuaded into conformity, or in social casework when such stereo-typical thinking as "a woman must stay home with her children" is forced on clients.

If social work stands for *cooperation* because it recognizes this as a basis for positive human relations, then highly competitive prac-tices inside an agency or among agencies become poor practice.

These examples show that a conscious value orientation can be helpful in research and in evaluation of social work practice.

5. How do we combine the concepts of self-determination and planning? This question is far less related to value determination than to an assertion of facts. Lindeman stated as one of his demo-cratic propositions, "Economic social and cultural planning are modern requisites for survival." This is not a value demand but rather a statement of what he considered a fact. Lindeman himself did not prove this, but all human history has shown that the more complicated a society becomes the more planning is necessary. The controversy between adherents of self-determination and adherents of planning has arisen mainly because of a lack of understanding of the two concepts. If self-determination is synonymous with laissez faire and planning is synonymous with authoritarian imposition, then the two concepts are contradictory. But if self-determination means the right to think and act for oneself as long as one does not interfere with the rights of others, and if planning is a thoughtful process of weighing different interests, then the two concepts are not contradictory but equally important and complementary. Theoretically, therefore, this question does not pose any contradictory alternatives.

In practice, solutions are not always easy because of vested interests and differences of opinion regarding planning. Social work considers both values — self-determination and planning — important and necessary in modern society. This is borne out in its recognition of three basic methods, casework, group work, and community organization, which present self-determination and planning. It is also expressed in the acceptance of the equal importance of public and private services.

6. *What is social work's relation to other professions?* Social work's basic values are mutual respect for people, interdependence, and cooperation; these point the way toward relationship with other professions. Social work has not always acted in accordance with those values. It has imitated other professions, looked down upon them, and competed with them. In reminding itself of its basic values it might establish more constructive relationships. The clarification of function itself does not lie in the realm of philosophy. It lies in the area of scientific approach to the problems of human beings and society as a whole and the question of how they will be served best and by whom. This clarification is a responsibility of every profession. Social work's specific responsibility should lie in its stress on cooperation instead of competition.

At present social work does not play this cooperative role. It is very status-conscious and competes with such professions as psychiatry and psychology. Two factors have helped to bring about these attitudes: (1) the aggressiveness of some of the other professions and (2) social work's increased realization that it has developed methods which can contribute to the improvement of human relations. Social work's consciousness of the values of interdependence and cooperation should help it to present its case with less competitiveness and more self-confidence while it assumes the role of the mediator so very necessary and important in a competitive society.

7. *What is the relation of the professional to the volunteer?* This question has plagued social work throughout its history. As a profession it grew out of the efforts of volunteers and it developed trained professionals only at a later period. With the development of professionals, controversy arose not only as to the respective functions of the two, but also as to their significance. In some areas of social work the volunteer was looked upon as an inferior, not just someone who performed a different function. Lindeman was greatly concerned with this question. He stressed the importance of enlightening the citizenry about all the problems with which social work dealt. He saw professionals and volunteers as partners who were equally informed and equally concerned with social work's goals, but each with a different function to fulfill. The volunteer was the one who kept alive community concern and who, in whatever capacity he served, brought to the social agency the live viewpoint of the layman. The social worker was the one who brought to the task the scientific knowledge and the skill to carry it out.

It is interesting to observe that during the 1920s and 1930s it seemed as if volunteer efforts would be appreciated mainly in the so-called group work field — the settlement houses and youth-serving agencies. In agencies concerned with casework, volunteers seemed to become less and less important. This has changed considerably with the growing interest in mental health. Citizens' organizations have become active as volunteers in mental hospitals and as fighters for services to the mentally retarded. A new partnership between intelligent citizens and social workers is permeating the social work field. It becomes increasingly important not to think of the volunteer as a money-raiser only, but to see him as a genuine partner in the effort for better social services.

To summarize: social work is a profession that presents a unique constellation of value, knowledge, and method. None of the three parts can be understood independent of the others.

Social work is based on the primary values of the dignity of the individual and the interdependence of human beings. Out of these grow basic "propositions" as Lindeman names them ("unity through diversity" or "consonance of ends and means") and basic principles underlying all its methods ("the social worker must start where client, group, or community is" or "the social worker must help client, group, community toward self-determination in accordance with the rights of others").

Social work is influenced by and uses in its practice secondary values. These must be constantly investigated with regard to their validity for the times, and each practitioner must become aware of his own values and how they originated in him.

Social work knowledge is based on many disciplines, with a trend toward increased integration and more emphasis on all areas of knowledge and more understanding of dynamics and interrelationships. Systems differ, but not basically; the differences concern researchable facts, not values.

Social work methods have in common basic goals and the values and principles derived from them. They differ in specific skills and intermediate goals. They must be evaluated in terms of their effectiveness as well as their consonance with the primary values.

The more the three social work methods are integrated and the more individual social workers gain knowledge of all three of them, the more the profession will be able to translate into practice the demands of individualization and cooperation.

The more social work realizes the clarification and acceptance of its inherent values, the more its practitioners will be called upon to investigate their practice in relation to those values. This will lead to *increased flexibility* (because of the change in secondary values on the basis of new facts) and *increased responsibility for social change.*

Evaluation of social work practice must be based on the use of latest knowledge and the adherence to primary values.

Research in social work can accept those primary values as axiomatic and move immediately into the investigation of facts.

Because of the demands it must make on its practitioners and on the community, social work must be very much aware of Lindeman's concept of the "partial functioning of ideals." Its *idealism must be realistic* and accept the fact that ideals can never be completely fulfilled. Recrimination among social workers is often based on the demand for "perfect" practice. Expectations are too often related to the ideal only. For example, schools are accused by agencies of not turning out perfect products, and agencies are accused by schools of not making perfect use of their products. The "partial functioning of ideals" concept implies the existence of and the striving toward ideals, but it recognizes the influence of reality.

The need for constant clarification of values in social work has implications for social work education. Though the primary values are axiomatic, they need constant new application to practice and they must be clarified and understood in the light of social work history. Students must learn about the religious and humanistic heritage and how it was applied or not applied in social work history. They must think through what value judgments are part of their practice. They must learn to see social work practice in this country and in other countries in the light of values, learn to compare them, learn to accept differing values and various applications of values, and build their conviction on knowledge and insight.

Social work has found that it can teach its methods only by constant analysis of them and by exercising them in practice. For this purpose students take part in method classes, seminars, and field work. Until now (with some exceptions) philosophy has been taught mostly by implication. Lindeman's great contribution was to point out the need for consciously learning and thinking through philosophical concepts. Without more seminars in philosophy (which must be in the form of inquiries, not dogmatic teaching), social work will continue its unstable swing from one extreme to another and its tendency to indoctrination. Schools of social work must offer thoughtful, free, and conscious investigation into philosophy related to social work.

Only if this content is added to the social work curriculum and if the profession is free to open inquiry based on respect for basic ethics will the social worker become, as Lindeman hoped in *Social Work as Human Relations*,

. . . something more than a skilled craftsman,
something more than a well-meaning idealist.

BIBLIOGRAPHY AND INDEX

BIBLIOGRAPHY

DURING the first half of 1955 the author had fifteen interviews with relatives and associates of Eduard C. Lindeman. She also had access to some of his correspondence, to letters written about him, and to unpublished manuscripts then in the possession of Mr. Robert Gessner and now in the possession of the New York School of Social Work. Especially valuable were the sixteen notebooks kept by Lindeman from 1937 to 1953, which Mr. and Mrs. Gessner graciously gave her permission to study; and an unpublished manuscript written by Lindeman in the last year of his life, "The New York School of Social Work — An Interpretative History," which is now in the possession of the New York School of Social Work.

Important background material to social work history was found in unpublished curriculum discussions in the possession of Clar A. Kaiser; in mimeographed material of the *Proceedings of the American Association of Schools of Social Work*, 1941–1950; in the *Manual of Accrediting*, 1943, of the same organization; and in the *Manual of Accrediting Standards* of the Council on Social Work Education, 1953.

All unpublished sources are indicated in the text.

Writings by Lindeman

"Adult Education for Social Changes," introduction to *A Handbook for Leaders and Members of Discussion Groups, Forums and Adult Classes*, Thomas K. Brown, Jr., ed., Swarthmore Seminar, Philadelphia, Pa., 1937.

"Agency Autonomy and Community Organization; Summary of Discussion," *Proceedings*, National Conference of Social Work, 1931.

"A Presidential Word, from Eduard C. Lindeman to Members of the National Conference of Social Work," *Conference Bulletin*, Summer 1952.

"A Venture in Fruit Growing Farther North," *The Gleaner*, XVIII, No. 2, November 1911.

"Basic Unities in Social Work," *Proceedings*, National Conference of Social Work, 1934.

The Church in the Changing Community. New York: The Community Church, 1929.

College Characters: Essays and Verse. Port Huron, Mich.: Riverside Printing Co., 1912.

The Community, An Introduction to the Study of Community Leadership and Organization. New York: Association Press, 1921.

"Community Responsibility to Our Peacetime Servicemen and Women," *Proceedings*, National Conference of Social Work, May 25–26, 1949.

"Cooperation Is the Next Step," *The Gleaner*, XVIII, No. 5, February 1912.
"Democracy and Social Work," *Proceedings*, National Conference of Social Work, 1948.
The Democratic Way of Life, with T. V. Smith, New York: New American Library of World Literature, 1951.
"Do We Need a New Approach to Democracy?" *Progressive Education*, XXV, No. 5, March 1948.
"Little Business and Big," review of *Concept of the Corporation*, by Peter Drucker, *Saturday Review of Literature*, XXIX, No. 30, July 27, 1946.
Dynamic Social Research, with John J. Hader. New York: Harcourt, 1933.
Review of *The Psychology of Human Society*, by Charles A. Elwood, *New Republic*, February 10, 1926.
"Emerging American Philosophy," *New Republic*, November 19, 1924.
Foreword to *Emerson, The Basic Writings of America's Sage*. New York: New American Library of World Literature, 1949.
"The Enduring Goal," *Survey Graphic*, November 1947.
A Fantasy, booklet. New York: YWCA, 1952.
"Foreign Students and International Understanding," *Bulletin*, New York School of Social Work, July 1946.
"From Social Work to Social Science," *New Republic*, June 2, 1926.
"Group Work and Democracy — A Philosophical Note," *New Trends in Group Work*, Joshua Lieberman, ed. New York: Association Press, 1938.
"Group Work and Education for Democracy," *Proceedings*, National Conference of Social Work, 1939.
"Housing and the Democratic Struggle," *Teachers College Record*, XL, No. 34–36, October 1942.
"The Human Situation," American Journal of Nursing, XXXIX, pp. 1315–21, December 1939.
"Industrial Technique and Social Assets," *Proceedings*, National Conference of Social Work, 1953.
"Industrial Technique and Social Ethics," *Proceedings*, National Conference of Social Work, 1923.
"Retribution and Causality," review of *Society and Nature: A Sociological Inquiry*, by Hans Kelan, *Christendom*, IX, No. 3, Summer 1944.
"Leadership: A Function of Democratic Experience," *Journal of Educational Sociology*, XVII, No. 7, March 1944.
Leisure — A National Issue. Planning for the Leisure of a Democratic People. New York: Association Press, 1939.
The Meaning of Adult Education. New York: New Republic, Inc., 1926.
Mental Hygiene and the Moral Crisis of Our Time. Austin: Univ. of Texas, Hogg Foundation, 1952.
"The Moral Sense of India," *Survey*, 1950.
"Morality for an Atomic Age," *New Leader*, XXVIII, No. 36, September 8, 1945.
"The Never-ending Struggle for Human Rights," *Alumni Newsletter*, New York School of Social Work, Summer 1948.
"New Patterns of Community Organization," *Proceedings*, National Conference of Social Work, 1937.
"New Trends in Community Control," *Proceedings*, National Conference of Social Work, 1932.
"Organization and Technique for Rural Recreation," *Proceedings*, National Conference of Social Work, 1920.

"Organization of Rural Social Forces," *Proceedings,* National Conference of Social Work, 1921.

"Palestine — Test of Democracy," *Christian Council on Palestine,* New York, 1945.

"Perspectives in Social Work," *Bulletin,* New York School of Social Work, July 1932.

"The Place of the Local Community in Organized Society," *Proceedings,* National Conference of Social Work, 1922.

"Planning: An Orderly Method for Social Change," *Annals of the American Academy of Political and Social Sciences,* July 1932.

"Pre-Point Four," *The Woman's Press,* September 1950.

"The Presidential Word," *Conference Bulletin,* National Conference of Social Work, Summer 1952.

"Recreation and the New Psychology," address given at the Recreation Congress, October 10, 1922; *The Playground,* July 1923.

"The Relation between Urban and Rural Social Work," *Proceedings,* National Conference of Social Work, 1924.

"Save the Grand Old Trees," *The Gleaner,* XVIII, No. 12, September 1915.

"Science and Philosophy: Sources of Humanitarian Faith," in *Social Work as Human Relations.* New York: Columbia Univ. Press, 1949.

Social Discovery. New York: Republic Publishing Co., 1924.

Social Education. New York: New Republic, Inc., 1933.

"Social Work Matures in a Confused World," *The Compass,* XXVIII, January 1947, pp. 3–9.

"The Social Worker and His Community," 24th New York State Conference of Charities, Rochester, November 13–15, 1923; *Survey Graphic,* LII, April 15, 1924, pp. 83–85.

"Some Mental Hygiene Factors in Community Processes," *Proceedings,* National Conference of Social Work, 1931.

"Sources of Value for Modern Man," *Religious Education,* September–October 1947.

Steps Toward Evaluating Progress in Private Social Agencies, Sixth Annual Board Members Institute. New York: Federation of Protestant Welfare Agencies, Inc., 1948.

"The Voice of the Concurring People," *University of Kansas City Review,* Winter 1951.

"What Are the Social Implications of the Cooperative Movement?" *Journal of Social Forces,* May 1923.

"What May a Professional School Reasonably Expect of Its Graduates?" *Bulletin,* Alumni Number, New York School of Social Work, July 1928.

Writings about Lindeman

Cohen, Nathan C. "E. C. Lindeman — The Teaching and Philosophy," *Proceedings,* National Conference of Social Work, 1953.

"Declaration of Principles," *The Gleaner,* XVIII, No. 5, February 1912.

Demorest, Charlotte K. "He Saw the Mountain in the Molehill," *20th Anniversary Yearbook of Adult Education, 1953,* New York Adult Education Council, 1953.

Detroit Free Press, Detroit, Mich., February 4, 1941.

Detroit News, Detroit, Mich., May 31, 1941.

Gessner, Robert, ed., *The Democratic Man.* Boston: Beacon Press, 1956.

Klein, Philip. "Discussion of Dr. Lindeman's Paper," *Proceedings*, National Conference of Social Work, 1921.
Slocum, Grant. Editorial in *The Gleaner*, XVII, No. 1, October 1911.
"The Survey Salutes . . ." *Survey*, October 1950.

Historical Background

Adams, James Truslow. *The Epic of America*. Boston: Little, Brown, 1932.
Allen, Frederick Lewis. *The Big Change*. New York: Harper, 1952.
Baron, Sale W. "American Jewish Communal Pioneering," *Publication of the American Jewish Historical Society*, XLIII, No. 3, March 1954.
Beard, Charles A., and Mary R. Beard. *A Basic History of the United States*. Philadelphia: Garden City Publishing Co., Inc., 1944.
Becker, Howard, and Harry Elmer Barnes. *Social Thought from Lore to Science*. Washington, D.C.: Harren Press, 1952.
Benét, Stephen Vincent. *Western Star*. New York: Farrar & Rinehart, Inc., 1943.
Bloch, Marc. *The Historian's Craft*. New York: Knopf, 1953.
Charnwood, Lord. *Theodore Roosevelt*. Boston: Atlantic Monthly Press, 1923.
Commager, Henry S. *The American Mind*. New Haven: Yale Univ. Press, 1950.
———, ed. *Documents of American History*. New York: Appleton-Century-Crofts, Inc., 1940.
———. *Living Ideas in America*. New York: Harper, 1951.
Croly, Herbert. *Willard Straight*. New York: Macmillan, 1924.
Curti, Merle. *Probing Our Past*. New York: Harper, 1955.
Deutsch, Albert. *Our Rejected Children*. Boston: Little, Brown, 1950.
———. *The Mentally Ill in America*. New York: Columbia Univ. Press, 1946.
Goldman, Eric F. *Rendezvous with Destiny, A History of Modern American Reform*. New York: Knopf, 1952.
Lasker, Bruno, ed. *Information Service*, IV, No. 11, March 14, 1925, Department of Research and Education, Federal Council of Churches of Christ in America.
Laski, Harold J. *The American Democracy*. New York: Viking Press, 1948.
———. *The American Presidency. An Interpretation*. New York: Harper, 1940.
MacIver, Robert M. "Sociology," *Encyclopedia of the Social Sciences*, XIV. New York: Macmillan, 1934.
Miller, J. Quinter. "Federal Council of the Churches of Christ in America," *Encyclopedia Americana*, XI. New York: Chicago Americana Corp., 1952.
Morison, Samuel Eliot, and Henry Steele Commager. *The Growth of the American Republic*, 2 vols. New York: Oxford Univ. Press, 1942.
Neuman, Abraham A. "The Evolving American Jewish Community," *The Jewish Social Service Quarterly*, XXXI, No. 1, Fall 1954.
Parrington, Vernon Louis. *Main Currents in American Thought*. New York: Harcourt, 1927.
Peterson, Florence. *American Labor Unions*. New York: Harper, 1952.
Toynbee, Arnold J. "The New Opportunity for Historians," Gideon Seymour Memorial Lecture, Univ. of Minnesota, November 6, 1955.
de Toqueville, Alexis. *Democracy in America*, 2 vols., Henry Reeve, tr. London: Saunders & Otley, 1835.

History of Social Work

Abbott, Edith. "Twenty-one Years of Education for the Social Services," *Social Service Review*, XV, December 1941.

"Edith Abbott," in *Current Biography*. New York: H. W. Wilson, 1941.

Abbott, Grace. *The Child and the State*, 2 vols. Chicago: Univ. of Chicago Press, 1938.

American Association of Schools of Social Work. *Summary and Findings of Four Workshops*. New York, 1952.

"Basic Problems and Issues," *Conference Bulletin*, National Conference of Social Work, LVIII, No. 4, Summer 1955.

Bruno, Frank J. *The Theory of Social Work*. Boston: Heath, 1936.

———. *Trends in Social Work*. New York: Columbia Univ. Press, 1948.

Council on Social Work Education. *Education for Social Work*. New York, 1953.

———. *Social Work Education in the Post-Master's Program*, No. 1. New York, 1953.

———. *Social Work Education in the Post-Master's Program*, No. 2. New York, 1953.

Coyle, Grace L. "Social Work at the Turn of the Decade," *Proceedings*, National Conference of Social Work, 1940.

Faulkner, Charles E. "Presidential Address," *Proceedings*, National Conference of Charities and Correction, 1900.

Fox, Hugh F. "Centralizing Tendencies in Administration," *Proceedings*, National Conference of Charities and Correction, 1900.

Friedlander, Walter A. *Introduction to Social Welfare*. New York: Prentice-Hall, Inc., 1955.

Hathway, Marion. "Twenty-five Years of Professional Education for Social Work," *Social Work Journal*, June 1946.

Hodges, George, D.D. "The Progress of Compassion," conference sermon, *Proceedings*, National Conference of Charities and Correction, 1901.

Hodson, William. "Is Social Work a Profession?" *Proceedings*, National Conference of Social Work, 1925.

Hopkins, C. Howard. *History of the YMCA in North America*. New York: Association Press, 1951.

Hopkins, Harry. "The National Program of Relief," *Proceedings*, National Conference of Social Work, 1933.

Kellogg, Paul U. *The Pittsburgh Survey*, 6 vols. New York: Russell Sage Foundation, 1914.

Klein, Philip. "Social Work," *Encyclopedia of the Social Sciences*, XIV. New York, Macmillan, 1935.

Lee, Porter R. *Social Work as Cause and Function*. New York: Columbia Univ. Press, 1937.

Queen, Stuart Alfred. *Social Work in the Light of History*. Philadelphia and London: Lippincott, 1922.

Richmond, Mary. "Charitable Cooperation," *Proceedings*, National Conference of Charities and Correction, 1900.

———. "Some Next Steps in Social Treatment," *Proceedings*, National Conference of Social Work, 1920.

Riis, Jacob A. "A Blast of Cheer," *Proceedings*, National Conference of Charities and Correction, 1900.

de Schweinitz, Karl. *England's Road to Social Security.* Philadelphia: University of Pennsylvania Press, 1943.

Taylor, Graham. *"Training of Social Workers,"* *Proceedings,* National Conference of Charities and Correction, 1905.

Tufts, James H. *Education and Training for Social Work.* New York: Russell Sage Foundation, 1923.

Warner, Amos G. *American Charities.* New York: Crowell, 1894, 1908, 1919.

Weller, G. F. *"Relief Work and Preventive Philanthropies as Related to Charity Organization,"* *Proceedings,* National Conference of Charities and Correction, 1902.

Wines, F. W. *"The Healing Touch,"* *Proceedings,* National Conference of Charities and Correction, 1900.

Woods, Robert A. *The Neighborhood in National Building.* Boston and New York: Houghton, 1925.

Philosophical Background

Adrian, Dr. E. D. *"Science and Human Nature,"* *World Mental Health,* Bulletin of the World Federation for Mental Health, February 1955.

Brinton, Crane. *Ideas and Men.* New York: Prentice-Hall, Inc., 1950.

Carlson, A. J. *"Does the Greater Understanding of Man and Nature Increase the Scientist's Social Responsibility?"* *Science,* CLXXVII, No. 3052, June 26, 1953.

Chase, Stuart. *The Human Sciences and the Arts of Practice.* New York: Columbia Univ. Press, 1949.

Dewey, John. *Democracy and Education.* New York: Macmillan, 1936.

——. *"Philosophy,"* in *Encyclopedia of the Social Sciences,* XII. New York: Macmillan, 1935.

——. *Reconstruction in Philosophy,* Eduard C. Lindeman, ed. New York: New American Library of World Literature, 1955.

Elwood, Charles A. *A History of Social Philosophy.* New York: Prentice-Hall, Inc., 1938.

Emerson, Ralph Waldo. *The Basic Writings of America's Sage,* Eduard C. Lindeman, ed. New York: New American Library of World Literature, 1949.

——. *Essays, Poems and Apothegms,* Eduard C. Lindeman, ed. New York: New American Library of World Literature, 1954.

Erikson, Erik H. *Childhood and Society.* New York: Norton, 1950.

——. *"Growth and Crisis of the 'Healthy Personality,'"* *Problems of Infancy and Childhood,* Supplement II. New York: Josiah Macy, Jr., Foundation, 1950.

Follett, Mary Parker. *Creative Experience.* New York: Longmans, 1924.

——. *Dynamic Administration,* Henry C. Metcalf and Lyndall F. Urwick, eds. New York: Harper, 1940.

——. *The New State, Group Organization. The Solution of Popular Government.* New York: Longmans, 1934.

Freud, Sigmund. *Moses and Monotheism,* Katherine Jones, tr. New York: Knopf, 1939.

——. *Psychoanalysis,* Joan Riviere, tr. New York: Modern Library, 1949.

Fromm, Erich. *Psychoanalysis and Religion.* New Haven: Yale Univ. Press, 1950.

Heilbronner, Robert L. *The Worldly Philosophers.* New York: Simon & Shuster, 1933.

James, William. *Essays on Faith and Morals,* selected by Ralph Barton Perry. New York, London, Toronto: Longmans, 1949.

———. *Essays in Pragmatism.* New York: Hafner Publishing Co., 1948.

Kant, Immanuel. *Critique of Pure Reason,* J. M. D. Meikeljohn, tr., rev. ed. New York: Willey Book Company, 1943.

Kluckhohn, Clyde, and Henry A. Murray, eds. *Personality in Nature, Society and Culture.* New York: Knopf, 1949.

Mead, George H. *Movements of Thought in the Nineteenth Century.* Chicago: Univ. of Chicago Press, 1936.

Mouroux, Jean. *The Meaning of Man,* A. M. G. Downes, tr. New York: Sheed & Ward, 1952.

Nelson, Leonard. *Socratic Method and Critical Philosophy, Selected Essays,* Thomas K. Brown, III, tr. New Haven: Yale Univ. Press, 1949.

Otto, Max. *Science and the Moral Life,* preface by Eduard C. Lindeman. New York: New American Library of World Literature, 1949.

Rauschenbusch, Walter. *Christianity and the Social Crisis.* New York: Macmillan, 1920.

Riesman, David. *The Lonely Crowd, A Study of the Changing American Character.* New Haven: Yale Univ. Press, 1950.

Russell, Bertrand. *A History of Western Philosophy.* New York: Simon & Shuster, 1945.

Schweitzer, Albert. *Kultur und Ethik.* Munich: C. H. Beck'sche Verlagsbuchhandlung, 1923.

———. *Verfall und Wiederaufbau der Kultur.* Munich: C. H. Beck'sche Verlagsbuchhandlung, 1923.

Stern, Karl. *The Third Revolution. A Study of Psychiatry and Religion.* New York: Harcourt, 1954.

Tufts, James Hayden. "What I Believe," in *Contemporary American Philosophers,* II. New York: Macmillan, 1930.

Voltaire. *Candide,* John Butt, tr. Baltimore: Penguin Classics, 1954.

Watson, John B. *Behaviorism.* New York: Norton, 1924–25.

Whitehead, Alfred North. *The Aims of Education and Other Essays.* London: Williams & Norgate, Ltd., 1950.

———. *Science and the Modern World.* New York: Macmillan, 1925.

Witmer, Helen Leland, and Ruth Kotinsky, eds. *Personality in the Making.* New York: Harper, 1952.

Philosophy of Social Work

Addams, Jane. "How Much Social Work Can a Community Afford: From the Ethical Point of View?" *Proceedings,* National Conference of Social Work, 1926.

American Association of Social Workers. *Standards for the Professional Practice of Social Work.* New York, 1951.

Austin, Lucille Nickel. "The Evolution of Our Social Case Work Concepts," *The Family,* XX, No. 2, April 1939.

Benne, Kenneth D., and G. E. Swanson, issue eds. "Values and the Social Scientist," *Journal of Social Issues,* VI, No. 4, 1950.

Bisno, Herbert. *The Philosophy of Social Work,* introduction by Eduard C. Lindeman. Washington, D.C.: Public Affairs Press, 1952.

Boehm, Werner. "The Role of Values in Social Work," *Jewish Social Service Quarterly*, XXVI, No. 4, June 1950.

———. "Social Work and the Social Sciences," *Journal of Psychiatric Social Work*, XXI, No. 1, September 1951.

Bowers, Rev. Père Swithun, O.M.I. "Formation en Service Social: un point de vue catholique," *Service Social*, I, No. 2, June 1951.

Bruno, Frank J. "Social Work Objectives in the New Era," presidential address, *Proceedings*, National Conference of Social Work, 1933.

Cannon, Antoinette. "Recent Changes in the Philosophy of Social Workers," *Proceedings*, National Conference of Social Work, 1933.

Cohen, Nathan E. "Desegregation — A Challenge to the Place of Moral Values in Social Work Education," in *Education for Social Work*. New York: Council on Social Work Education, 1955.

Cooke, Rev. Terence J. *Thomistic Philosophy in the Principles of Social Group Work*. Washington, D.C.: Catholic Univ. Press, 1951.

Edman, Irwin. "Contribution of the Humanities and the Professional Schools," in *Social Work as Human Relations*. New York: Columbia Univ. Press, 1949.

Hailman, David E. "A Code of Ethics for the Social Worker," *Social Work Journal*, XXX, No. 2, April 1949.

Hall, L. K. "Group Work and Professional Ethics," *The Group*, XV, No. 1.

Hamilton, Gordon. "Helping People — The Growth of a Profession," in *Social Work as Human Relations*. New York: Columbia Univ. Press, 1949.

———. "The Underlying Philosophy of Casework Today," *Proceedings*, National Conference of Social Work, 1941.

Johnson, Arlien. "Educating Professional Social Workers for Ethical Practice," *Social Service Review*, XXIX, No. 2, June 1955.

de Jongh, J. F. "Self-Help in Modern Society," *Social Work Journal*, XXXV, No. 4, October 1954.

Kardiner, Abram. "Security, Cultural Restraints, Intrasocial Dependence and Hostilities," *The Family*, XVIII, No. 6, October 1937.

Kasius, Cora, ed. *New Directions in Social Work*. New York: Harper, 1954.

Kidneigh, John C. "People, Problems and Plans," *Social Service Review*, XXV, No. 2, June 1951.

Konopka, Gisela. "The Application of Social Work Principles to International Relations," *Proceedings*, National Conference of Social Work, 1953.

Kraus, Hertha. "The Future of Social Work: Some Comments on Social Work Function," *The Compass*, XXIX, No. 1, January 1948.

Lovejoy, Owen R. "Standards of Living and Labor," *Proceedings*, National Conference of Social Work, 1912.

McCormick, Mary J. *Diagnostic Casework in the Thomistic Pattern*. New York: Columbia Univ. Press, 1954.

Mayo, Leonard W. "The Government and the People: Conflict or Partnership," *Survey*, February 1949.

Niebuhr, Reinhold. *The Contribution of Religion to Social Work*. New York: Columbia Univ. Press, 1932.

Reynolds, Bertha C. *Social Work and Social Living*. New York: Citadel Press, 1951.

Sorenson, Ray, and Hedley S. Dimock. *Designing Education in Values*. New York: Association Press, 1955.

Stidley, Leonard Albert. *Sectarian Welfare Federation among Protestants*. New York: Association Press, 1944.

Todd, Arthur James. *The Scientific Spirit and Social Work*. New York: Macmillan, 1920.

Towley, Louis H. "Professional Responsibility in a Democracy," *Proceedings*, Council of Social Work Education; Education for Social Work, 1953.

Van Waters, Miriam. "New Morality and Social Workers," *Proceedings*, National Conference of Social Work, 1929.

———. "Philosophical Trends in Modern Social Work," *Proceedings*, National Conference of Social Work, 1930.

Wilson, Gertrude. "Human Needs Pertinent to Group Work Services," *Proceedings*, National Conference of Social Work, 1942.

Youngdahl, Benjamin E. "Social Work at the Crossroads," *Social Work Journal*, XXXIV, No. 3, July 1953.

Practice of Social Work

Ackerman, Nathan W. "Mental Hygiene and Social Work, Today and Tomorrow," *Social Casework*, XXXVI, No. 2, February 1955.

Addams, Jane. *The Spirit of Youth and the City Streets*. New York: Macmillan, 1909.

———. "The Call of the Social Field," *Proceedings*, National Conference of Social Work, 1911.

"Basic Problems and Issues," *Conference Bulletin*, National Conference of Social Work, LVIII, No. 4, Summer 1955.

Beveridge, Right Hon. Lord. "The Function of a School of Social Science," *World Mental Health*, VII, No. 1, February 1955.

Bowers, Swithun, O.M.I. "The Nature and Definition of Social Casework," *Journal of Social Casework*, 1949.

Burns, Eveline M. "The Role of Government in Social Welfare," *Social Work Journal*, XXXV, No. 3, July 1954.

Cohen, Nathan E. "Preview: The Field of Social Work," *Alumni Newsletter*, New York School of Social Work, Fall 1951.

Coyle, Grace Longwell. *Group Work with American Youth*. New York: Harper, 1948.

———. "Proposed Areas for Concentration and Study," *The Group*, XVII, No. 5, June 1955.

———. "Social Group Work," *Social Work Yearbook, 1954*. New York: American Association of Social Workers, 1954.

"Education for Social Work," *Proceedings*, 3rd Annual Program Meeting, Council on Social Work Education, Chicago, January 26–29, 1955. New York: Council on Social Work Education, 1955.

Fink, Arthur E. *Field of Social Work*. New York: Holt, 1949.

Flexner, Abraham. "Is Social Work a Profession?" *Proceedings*, National Conference of Charities and Correction, 1915.

Glasser, Melvin A. "Social Work in 1954: Potentialities and Pitfalls," *Social Work Journal*, XXXV, No. 3, July 1954.

Greenwood, Ernest. *Toward a Sociology of Social Work*. Welfare Council of Metropolitan Los Angeles, Special Report Series No. 37, 1953.

Group Work Horizons, Selected Papers for the Year 1944. Reports by Committees of the Association for 1943–44. New York: Association Press, 1944.

Hamilton, Gordon. "Role of Social Case Work in Social Policy," *Social Case Work*, XXXIII, No. 8, October 1952.

——. *Theory and Practice of Social Work.* New York: Columbia Univ. Press, 1940.

Hoey, Jane M. "The Contribution of Social Work to Government," *Proceedings,* National Conference of Social Work, 1941.

Hollis, Ernest V., and Alice L. Taylor. *Social Work Education in the United States.* New York: Columbia Univ. Press, 1951.

Howard, Donald. "The Common Core of Social Work in Different Countries," *Social Work Journal,* XXXII, No. 4, October 1951.

Kahn, Alfred J. *A Court for Children.* New York: Columbia Univ. Press, 1953.

Kaiser, Clara A. "Group Work Education in the Last Decade," *The Group,* XV, No. 5, June 1953.

Kasius, Cora, ed. *A Comparison of Diagnostic and Functional Casework Concepts.* Report of the Family Service Association of America, Committee to Study Basic Concepts in Casework Practice. New York: Family Service Association, 1950.

Klein, Philip, and Ida C. Merrian. *The Contribution of Research to Social Work.* New York: American Association of Social Workers, 1948.

Konopka, Gisela. *Group Work in the Institution — A Modern Challenge.* New York: Whiteside, Inc., 1954.

McCaskill, Joseph C. *Theory and Practice of Group Work.* New York: Association Press, 1930.

McMillen, Wayne. *Community Organization for Social Welfare.* Chicago: Univ. of Chicago Press, 1945.

McNeil, C. F. "Community Organization for Social Welfare," *Social Work Yearbook,* 1954. New York: American Association of Social Workers, 1954.

Milford Conference Report. *Social Case Work, Generic and Specific.* New York: American Association of Social Workers, 1929.

The Nature and Definition of Social Case Work. New York: Family Service Association of America, 1949.

Newstetter, W. I. "What Is Social Group Work?" *Proceedings,* National Conference of Social Work, 1925.

Norton, William J. "What Is Social Work?" *Proceedings,* National Conference of Social Work, 1925.

Peck, J., and C. Plotkin. "Social Caseworkers in Private Practice," degree project, New York School of Social Work, April 1950.

Perkins, Frances. "The Evolving Task of Social Work," *Social Work Journal,* XXXII, No. 1, January 1951.

Reynolds, Bertha C. *Learning and Teaching in the Practice of Social Work.* New York: Harper, 1948.

Richmond, Mary. "The Social Case Worker's Task," *Proceedings,* National Conference of Social Work, 1917.

——. *Social Diagnosis,* 3rd ed. New York: Russell Sage Foundation, 1917.

Sheffield, Alfred Dwight. *Joining in Public Discussion, A Study of Effective Speechmaking for Members of Labor Unions, Conferences, Forums, and Other Discussion Groups.* New York: George H. Doran Co., 1922.

Sims, Newell Leroy. *The Rural Community.* New York: Scribner, 1920.

Smalley, Ruth. "Can We Reconcile Generic Education and Specialized Practice?" *Social Welfare Forum,* 1953.

Sullivan, Dorothea F., ed. *Readings . . . in Group Work.* New York: Association Press, 1952.

Toward Professional Standards. New York: American Association of Group Workers, 1947.

Towle, Charlotte. *Common Human Needs.* Federal Security Agency, Public Assistance Report No. 6, 1945.

———. "The Distinctive Attributes of Education for Social Work," *Social Work Journal,* XXXIII, No. 2, April 1952.

Trecker, Harleigh B., ed. *Group Work in the Psychiatric Setting.* New York: Whiteside, Inc. and William Marrows Co., 1956.

———. *Social Group Work,* 2nd ed. New York: Whiteside, Inc., 1955.

———, Frank C. Glick, and John C. Kidneigh. *Education for Social Work Administration.* New York: American Association of Social Workers, 1952.

Warren, Muriel A. "The Teaching Function of the Case Worker," degree project, New York School of Social Work, July 1933.

Wilson, Gertrude, and Gladys Ryland. *Social Group Work Practice.* Boston: Houghton, 1949.

Witmer, Helen L. *Social Work, An Analysis of a Social Institution.* New York: Farrar, 1942.

INDEX

Abbott, Edith, 37
Addams, Jane, 27, 90, 100, 122
Adjustment, theory of: question of value raised, 6, 101; answer proposed, 196
Adler, Felix, 39
Adolescents: misunderstood, 182; develop sense of identity, 191; form group associations, 192
American Association for the Study of Group Work, 129
American Association of Social Workers: *1951* meeting, 179, 183, 186; mentioned, 100
American Recreation Association, 27
Arnold, Mary, 48
Association of Training Schools for Professional Social Workers, 38
Austin, Lucille, "The Evolution of Our Casework Concepts," 54–55

Baldwin, Roger, 17, 64, 75–77
Beard, Charles, 39
Beers, Clifford, *A Mind that Found Himself*, 91
Behaviorism, 111–12
Bisno, Herbert, *Philosophy of Social Work*, 168–70
Bowers, Swithun, 175, 186, 187
Boy Scouts, 90
Brennack, Father Thomas, 44, 48
Bruno, Frank, 97, 128

Campfire Girls, 90
Cannon, Antoinette: 48; "Recent Changes in the Philosophy of Social Workers," 133–35
Carter, E. C., 39
Casework: functional school opposes

diagnostic school, 54; origin of, 94–95; makes use of psychiatry, 98; challenged by group work concepts, 99–101
Catholic Church and a philosophy of social work, 169–70
Catholic social workers subject to conflict in secondary values, 183–84
Catholic Youth Organization (CYO), 90
"Century of the Child," 91
Charity: idea of gives way to social justice, 84–96; religious motivation for, 85–86
Charity Organization Society, 88
Child Welfare, 6, 91–92
Children's Bureau, 92
Christianity, attitudes toward the poor, 86
Civil liberties: in wartime, 65; in postwar U.S., 68; McCarthyism, 152
Civil rights, 140–41, 142
Claghorn, Kate, 46
Club work, 96
Cohen, Nathan: 3–4; "Eduard C. Lindeman — The Teaching and Philosophy," 170–71
Commager, Henry S., 88
Community audits proposed by Lindeman, 140–41
Community organization analyzed early by Lindeman in *The Community*, 102–9
Cooke, Father Terence J., *Thomistic Philosophy in the Principles of Social Group Work*, 166–68
Correctional field, reforms in, 91
Cotton, Thomas, 50